Hack the Cybersecurity Interview

A complete interview preparation guide for jumpstarting your cybersecurity career

Ken Underhill

Christophe Foulon

Tia Hopkins

BIRMINGHAM—MUMBAI

Hack the Cybersecurity Interview

Copyright © 2022 Packt Publishing

Group Product Manager: Vijin Boricha

Publishing Product Manager: Mohd Riyan Khan

Senior Editor: Athikho Sapuni Rishana

Content Development Editor: Sayali Pingale

Technical Editor: Arjun Varma

Copy Editor: Safis Editing

Associate Project Manager: Neil Dmello

Proofreader: Safis Editing

Indexer: Subalakshmi Govindhan

Production Designer: Alishon Mendonca

Marketing Coordinator: Sourodeep Sinha

Senior Marketing Coordinator: Hemangi Lotlikar

First published: July 2022

Production reference: 1010722

Published by Packt Publishing Ltd.

Livery Place

35 Livery Street

Birmingham

B3 2PB, UK.

978-1-80181-663-2

www.packt.com

I would like to thank my wife for her continued patience and support as I work to make the cyber world a better place. No amount of the impact I've had on millions of people around the world would be possible without her. I would also like to thank all of my students and the people that I have helped with their cybersecurity careers over the years. Your messages of gratitude remind me of why I do what I do. I would also like to thank my long-time business coaches Ed Hoffman and David Wells, PhD, for pushing me past the limitations in my head. As you read this book and grow your successful cybersecurity career, don't forget to reach a hand back to help others with their journey.

– Ken Underhill

I would like to thank my wife and son, who support me in all my extra-curricular activities supporting the cybersecurity community, from writing books like this to coaching and podcasts. They are my rock and support when times are tough and are always there for me.

– Christophe Foulon

I would like to thank my mother for all the sacrifices she made to ensure I grew up to be a strong and empowered woman. My confidence, resilience, and grit are the direct result of the incredible example she set for me and the values she instilled in me. It is because of her that I have the strength to push forward in the face of adversity. I would also like to thank everyone in the cybersecurity community and beyond who has connected with me over the years to thank me for the impact I've had on their lives and their career journeys. My goal is to always lift as I climb, so it means a great deal to me to know that my efforts and influence are yielding positive results.

– Tia Hopkins

Foreword

To the reader,

When Ken asked me to write this foreword, I jumped at the chance to do so. I have had my share of formal and informal interviews, virtually and in person. My first interview was for a network engineer role at a three-letter agency in the DC area. However, this experience didn't stop me from learning.

Over time, my research and preparation skills improved significantly, landing me various roles, from information security analyst to vulnerability management engineer to sales engineering (technical presales), but having a resource that is concise is gold! In addition, it helps make the interview process a little easier and much more enjoyable.

The authors of this book, Tia, Chris, and Ken, have a plethora of knowledge in various areas of cybersecurity. They are the go-to people for breaking into cyber and advancing in cybersecurity. They focus on different cyber domains, but collectively, they have one goal: to bring more diversity into this field. These three are not only great at what they do but want to see people succeed, and I am happy to call them friends!

On average, only about 20% of applicants for a job will make it to the interview stage. So, when you get to the interview stage, you should probably research questions and how to answer them. If you are reading this book, be prepared. There isn't any fluff. Tia, Chris, and Ken give it to you straight with a bit of humor to keep the mood light. You will find differing experiences for the various roles highlighted in the book and some great things to consider when preparing for your interview. The authors even go as far as providing a framework that you can use to be successful. So, take this book, read what you need, and apply the techniques recommended.

Happy reading,

Mari Galloway

CEO, Founding Board Member

Women's Society of Cyberjutsu

Contributors

About the authors

Ken Underhill is the executive producer and host of the syndicated Cyber Life® television show, which reaches millions of viewers each month around the world on the Binge Networks app, Amazon, Roku, and over 100 other streaming television channels. He has won multiple industry awards for his work to improve diversity in the industry and is an advocate for women's rights. Ken educates around 2.6 million people each year through his online cybersecurity courses, is an executive and business owner, and sits on the advisory board of **Breaking Barriers Women in Cybersecurity (BBWIC)** and the Whole Cyber Human Initiative, along with sitting on the board for a number of cybersecurity start-up companies.

> *I would like to thank my co-authors, Chris and Tia, for agreeing to do this book and sharing their wisdom with the world. I would also like to thank Mari Galloway for agreeing to join us on this book journey. Thanks to our technical editors for surfacing new perspectives as we wrote this book.*

Christophe Foulon, senior manager and cybersecurity consultant at F10 FinTech, brings over 15 years of experience as a vCISO, information security manager, adjunct professor, author, and cybersecurity strategist with a passion for customer service, process improvement, and information security. He also has spent more than 10 years leading, coaching, and mentoring people. As a security practitioner, Christophe is focused on helping businesses tackle their cybersecurity risks while minimizing friction, resulting in increased resiliency, and aiding to secure people and processes with a solid understanding of the technology involved. He also hosts the Breaking into Cybersecurity podcast and co-authored *Develop Your Cybersecurity Career Path*.

I would like to acknowledge the staff, editors, and co-authors who have guided me through the process of writing this book. I would also like to thank the readers of these books who support authors like us and then give back by helping those who follow behind them by recommending resources and sharing experiences to keep this cycle going.

Tia Hopkins is the field CTO and chief cyber risk strategist at eSentire. She is also an adjunct professor of cybersecurity at Yeshiva University, a football coach, and is pursuing an executive MBA and Ph.D. in cybersecurity.

Tia was recognized by SC Media as an outstanding educator in 2019, as well as one of the Top 25 Women Leaders in Cybersecurity and Top 100 Women in Cybersecurity, both in 2020. In 2021, Tia was recognized as a Top Influencer in the Security Executives category by IFSEC Global. She also contributed a chapter to the book *The Rise of Cyber Women: Volume 2*.

Tia is the founder of Empow(H)er Cybersecurity, a non-profit organization aimed at inspiring and empowering women of color to pursue cybersecurity careers.

I would like to thank Ken for inviting me to join him and Chris on this amazing journey. I would also like to thank all of our supporters for believing in the value of this book, and I look forward to your feedback on how it helped you in your cybersecurity career journey. Don't forget to pay it forward!

About the reviewers

Linda W. Bell, CISSP, CDPSE, is a security architect and compliance lead for IBM Security Verify, with over 15 years of experience in risk management and accounting. After serving as a cybersecurity engineer in the Global CISO organization, she transitioned to resiliency advisor in the IBM Security BISO. There, she provided expertise in business continuity program management and incident response. Linda is a sought-after speaker on security topics and has been interviewed by several publications and organizations. Outside of work, Linda mentors underrepresented groups to help them attain certifications or training for STEM-based careers. She holds a Bachelor of Science degree in information technology from the University of South Florida.

> *I'd like to thank my family for supporting me over my career. Technology requires lifelong learning to stay current and I appreciate their patience when I am studying over weekends or for certifications. Also, a big thanks to all the women who sent the elevator back down and opened doors for me to be able to tell my STEMstory.*

Louis Anthony Maldonado Jr has worked in various areas of cybersecurity. As a lead analyst for critical infrastructure at Duke-Energy, Louis has stood up and matured command centers, directed EDR assessments overseas, and trained global security operations centers on monitoring and response. He was a consultant at multiple international agencies representing SOAR integrations and automation for various clients. Currently at Pacific Gas and Electric across the United States and back in critical infrastructure, Louis is maturing his department's cybersecurity posture. Louis is a leader among his peers and has a strong presence in the industry.

> *I'd like to thank my mother, Patricia, who never gave up on me and continued to push me to pursue my passion. Thanks to my two boys, Louis and James, as they unknowingly fueled my career and growth. Thanks to the authors of this book, allowing others to obtain this knowledge and grow their careers. Thanks to my colleague George from Blak Cyber, who referred me to Packt, and my contacts at Packt who kept me focused. Cheers!*

Table of Contents

3

Penetration Tester

4

Digital Forensic Analyst

5

Cryptographer/Cryptanalyst

6

GRC/Privacy Analyst

7

Security Auditor

8

Malware Analyst

Part 3: Cybersecurity Management Careers and Interview Questions

9

Cybersecurity Manager

10

Cybersecurity Sales Engineer

11

CISO

12

Behavioral Interview Questions

13

Final Thoughts

Index

Other Books You May Enjoy

Preface

This book covers best practices for preparing yourself for cybersecurity job interviews. Most of the chapters cover a specific cybersecurity job and interview questions that you might be asked in the interview. The behavioral interview questions chapter covers questions the authors have been asked during interviews, regardless of job role. The final chapter of the book covers additional information from the authors on how to best prepare yourself for job interviews. Remember, your resume and networking with people can get you the interview, but preparation for the interview is what helps you get the job.

Who this book is for

This book is valuable to aspiring cybersecurity professionals looking to gain an insight into the types of questions they might face during an interview. It's also for experienced cybersecurity professionals looking to level up their interview game.

What this book covers

Chapter 1, Hacking Yourself, is where you are going to learn about tips on preparing for your job interview, some general interview questions you might be asked and how you should respond to them, and ways to handle stress.

Chapter 2, SOC Analyst, is where you will learn about the SOC analyst career path and some of the common interview questions that are asked.

Chapter 3, Penetration Tester, is where you will learn about the penetration tester career path and some of the common interview questions that are asked.

Chapter 4, Digital Forensics Analyst, is where you will learn about the digital forensic analyst career path and some of the common interview questions that are asked.

Chapter 5, Cryptographer/Cryptanalyst, is where you will learn about the cryptographer career path and some of the common interview questions that are asked.

Chapter 6, GRC/Privacy Analyst, is where you will learn about the GRC analyst career path and some of the common interview questions that are asked.

Chapter 7, Security Auditor, is where you will learn about the security auditor career path and some of the common interview questions that are asked.

Chapter 8, Malware Analyst, is where you will learn about the malware analyst career path and some of the common interview questions that are asked.

Chapter 9, Cybersecurity Manager, is where you will learn about the cybersecurity manager career path and some of the common interview questions that are asked.

Chapter 10, Cybersecurity Sales Engineer, is where you will learn about the cybersecurity sales engineer career path and some of the common interview questions that are asked.

Chapter 11, CISO, is where you will learn about the **Chief Information Security Officer** (**CISO**) career path and some of the common interview questions that are asked.

Chapter 12, Behavioral Interview Questions, is where you will learn some of the most common behavioral interview questions that are asked across cybersecurity career paths. This chapter is a must-read for anyone looking to be successful in their interview.

Chapter 13, Final Thoughts, is where we, the authors, share our final advice to help you succeed in both your job interview and in your cybersecurity career.

To get the most out of this book

To get the most out of this book, it's important to understand why you want to work in cybersecurity and to practice for your job interview. We suggest writing out the questions that you think the interviewer will ask you based on the job you are applying for, then do your best to answer those questions. Doing this will help you during the job interview, ensuring that you are not stumbling around for answers to the interviewers' questions.

This book is not intended to be read cover to cover, although you can do that. Instead, we suggest that you read *Chapter 1, Hacking Yourself, Chapter 12, Behavioral Interview Questions,* and *Chapter 13, Final Thoughts,* and then read only the chapters for the job roles that you are applying to. The information in all chapters will be beneficial to you, but by focusing on the job interview that is in front of you, you will be in a much better position to succeed. For example, if you are interviewing for a SOC analyst job, the chapter on CISO interview questions will still be informative, but your main focus should be on the SOC analyst interview questions, since that is the job interview you have next week.

After reading this book, it's critical that you actually apply the knowledge. People often say knowledge is power, but in reality, applied knowledge is the real superpower. The more you practice for your job interview in advance, the easier the job interview usually is.

Also, after you apply the information in this book and do well in your job interview, please share a post on social media and tag the authors because we care about your success and want to see your wins.

Download the color images

We also provide a PDF file that has color images of the screenshots/diagrams used in this book. You can download it here: `https://static.packt-cdn.com/downloads/9781801816632_ColorImages.pdf`.

Conventions used

There are a few text conventions used throughout this book.

`Code in text`: Indicates code words in text, database table names, folder names, filenames, file extensions, pathnames, dummy URLs, user input, and Twitter handles. Here is an example: "You can use the `sleep` command, and if the web app sleeps for a period of time, it could indicate that it is vulnerable."

> **Tips or Important Notes**
> Appear like this.

Get in touch

Feedback from our readers is always welcome.

General feedback: If you have questions about any aspect of this book, mention the book title in the subject of your message and email us at `customercare@packtpub.com`.

Errata: Although we have taken every care to ensure the accuracy of our content, mistakes do happen. If you have found a mistake in this book, we would be grateful if you would report this to us. Please visit `www.packtpub.com/support/errata`, selecting your book, clicking on the Errata Submission Form link, and entering the details.

Piracy: If you come across any illegal copies of our works in any form on the Internet, we would be grateful if you would provide us with the location address or website name. Please contact us at `copyright@packt.com` with a link to the material.

If you are interested in becoming an author: If there is a topic that you have expertise in and you are interested in either writing or contributing to a book, please visit `authors.packtpub.com`.

Share Your Thoughts

Once you've read *Hack the Cybersecurity Interview*, we'd love to hear your thoughts!
Scan the QR code below to go straight to the Amazon review page for this book and share
your feedback.

https://packt.link/r/1801816638

Your review is important to us and the tech community and will help us make sure we're
delivering excellent quality content.

Part 1:
Hacking Yourself

This part introduces you to the book, the H.A.C.K. method, fundamental negotiation skills, and stress management.

This part of the book comprises the following chapter:

- *Chapter 1, Hacking Yourself*

1
Hacking Yourself

In this chapter, you will learn how to use this book, especially if you only have a short period of time before your job interview. You will also learn about some of the most common job interview questions asked and recommendations for how to answer them. This chapter also covers a brief introduction to personal branding and a simple method for reducing stress before a job interview.

The following topics will be covered in this chapter:

- How to get the most out of this book
- General interview advice
- Common interview questions
- Definition of cybersecurity
- The **How, Analyze, Collect, and Know (HACK)** method
- Personal branding and soft skills
- Negotiation 101
- Managing stress

How to get the most out of this book

If you're reading this book and only have a short time before your job interview, let me share some wisdom on how to get the most out of it.

This book is not intended to be read from cover to cover, although it can be.

I would suggest reading through at least *Part 1* (*Hacking Yourself*) and *Part 4* (*Common Behavioral Interview Questions*), plus the individual job role that you're interviewing for (assuming it's one listed in this book).

Many of the behavioral interview questions near the back of this book have been asked in interviews I've done, and some of the questions may be asked verbatim in your interview. This is why it's important to prepare for your interview.

I want to stress that the technology mentioned in this book will likely change over the years, so the technical interview questions should not be taken as a *Holy Grail* guide but rather as a more general guide to the types of questions an employer may ask you during an interview. Also, you may see questions on various tools that are used in each job role.

The questions you get about tools in an interview depend a lot on the company you are interviewing with and the tools they use.

The most important thing to remember is that having an understanding of the type of tool (that is, **security information and event management (SIEM)**, **endpoint detection and response (EDR)**, fuzzer, and so on) is more important than trying to get experience with every tool out there (it's impossible to be an expert in everything).

I also want to mention that this book could not possibly cover every possible interview question you might get (and I've had some strange questions asked of me over the years), but I've made every effort to include some of the most common ones after interviewing hundreds of cybersecurity professionals in these roles and going through hundreds of interviews myself over the years.

General interview advice

Your words have power.

As corny as that statement might sound to you, I've found in life that statement is true.

I remember a few years ago, I needed to get my driver's license renewed and saw over 100 people waiting in front of me in the ticketing system line.

The first thought in my head was: *This is going to take all day.*

But what I said out loud to myself was: *This line is going to move quickly, and they will call my ticket number in less than 20 minutes. In fact, people ahead of me in line are going to comment that this is the fastest they've ever seen the line move.*

Guess what happened.

Yes—you are correct.

The line moved quickly, and my ticket number was called in about 15 minutes. A few people ahead of me in line also commented how they had never seen the line move that quickly.

Am I claiming some superhero power, or am I planning to dive into a deep metaphysical discussion here?

Not at all—and I would much rather have the ability to freeze someone with ice as a superpower, anyways.

However, this is an example of the power of your words. You can search online and across social media platforms to see thousands of other examples of this.

There are also numerous books on the subject. A great one I've read is *What to Say When You Talk to Yourself* by Shad Helmstetter.

It's important to speak the right way before any job interview. Instead of saying things such as *I'm dumb* or *They will hate me*, say things such as *This is going to be a great interview. Everyone is going to be friendly to me and the questions they ask will be easy. In fact, it will feel more like a conversation with old friends than a job interview.*

Now, does this guarantee you will ace the interview and get the job? No—of course not. And sometimes, you don't get certain jobs because something much better for you is right around the corner. I have even experienced this in the past.

Common interview questions

Now, let's look at some common interview questions I've gotten over the years. I've been asked the following:

- **Who are you? (also known as, Tell me about yourself)**

  I've always wanted to answer this question with *I'm Batman,* but for some reason, I suspected the interviewer would not find that funny and I really needed the job at the time.

  This question is not a place for you to share your childhood memories and how your mom didn't hug you enough.

Instead, what the interviewer wants to hear is a brief summary of your career with a focus on your *impact* on past employers. Think of this as your 30-second elevator pitch.

Here's an example:

From the job posting, it's clear the person in this **Security Operations Center (SOC)** analyst role needs to be ready to go on day one and deliver results fast. That's what I've been able to do at *Acme Inc.* I developed a new SIEM tool for them within 60 days of hire and created an automation program that reduced false positives by 12%. Would you like to hear more about anything I've mentioned so far?

- **What is your greatest strength?**

  Under the section titled *The HACK method* later in this chapter, we'll talk about analyzing yourself. This *greatest strength* question is where you can focus on your key value points and how you are the right fit for the position.

  Here's an example:

  I would say my greatest strength is the ability to break down technical information and present it in an easily digestible format for stakeholders across an organization.

- **What is your greatest weakness?**

  With this question, I would typically just bring up a weakness they already know about and then end with some of the value I bring to an organization. *I work too hard* would be a dumb answer here. The interviewer is typically trying to assess your self-awareness with this question.

  Here's an example:

  I would say my greatest weakness is that I don't have the required 27 years of Kubernetes experience, **Certified Information Systems Security Professional (CISSP)** certification, and 19 PhDs required in the job description for this entry-level cybersecurity position, but I did reduce support tickets by 14% in my last position, which saved *Acme Inc* over $57,000 **United States dollars (USD)**.

- **Why are you leaving your current job?**

  You should not answer this question with *Because my boss sucks*. I usually would answer this one with something about growing your career in a new role.

  Here's an example:

  While I've enjoyed my time at *Acme Inc*, I realized it was time to move to the next level in my career as a pentester.

- **Where do you see yourself in (x) years?**

This one is usually asked as *Where do you see yourself in 5 years?* Some people will tell you to answer *I see myself working in your position*, which is a dumb idea in my opinion. That puts the interviewer on the defense, and you want to keep them relaxed and liking you. I used to answer this one and then ask the interviewer a question. The more you can keep the interview a conversation and not an interview, the better off you are.

Here's an example:

For the next 5 years, I see myself growing in my skillset and taking on more responsibility in the organization. Can you tell me how other SOC analysts have advanced their careers at the company?

- **What are your salary expectations?**

Everyone hates this one. I typically would start by thanking them for the question and then mentioning if everyone decides it's a good match, we can discuss compensation at that time. You can also ask the interviewer directly what the salary range is for the position to see if they are willing to share it. Some companies out there require the interviewer to get an actual base salary number, so in those instances, I would usually quote 30-40% above what you're making now. Yes—that might get you disqualified from the job, but if they can't pay you a fair wage, why would you ever want to work there?

Here are a few examples:

I appreciate you asking me that question. Would you be against us discussing compensation after everyone has agreed that this is a good match?

I appreciate you asking that question. Are you needing a minimum salary number for your interview form?

Assuming they answer yes (most interviewers will be honest about this), then give them a number 30-40% above your current base salary.

Here are some interview questions I think you should ask:

- **Which key performance indicators (KPIs) would you have for me in this position over the first 30, 60, and 90 days?**

  This question does a few things that benefit you. First, it gets the interviewer thinking of you in the position and not other candidates. Second, it lets you know what is expected of you in the position over the next 90 days. If the interviewer (assuming it's the hiring manager) has not thought about any KPIs for the position, it might indicate they are overwhelmed with work, and it might not be a good company for you.

- **What kind of person succeeds at this company?**

  This helps you understand how the company defines success. If the answer is someone that works 100-hour weeks, then you should probably run out of that interview as fast as you can.

- **What do you enjoy most about working at this company?**

  If the interviewer is happy in their role, then they might share a few things they love. On the other hand, by asking this question, you might be able to save yourself some headaches from working in a toxic environment. It's amazing what some interviewers will share with you if you ask the right questions (social engineering at its finest).

- **What do you see as my greatest strengths for this position?**

  This question is another way to keep the interviewer thinking about you for the position over others. And if they don't have any strengths to share, it's highly unlikely you have a chance at getting the job, so you save yourself some stress in waiting to hear back.

Here are a few other tips for your interview:

- **Make eye contact**: I would say you want to make eye contact most of the time when you're listening to the interviewer and when you're answering questions. Little or no eye contact can make people suspicious and feel you're not trustworthy.

- **Smile more**: Don't be creepy with this one, though. If someone is constantly smiling in the interview, I immediately feel it's not genuine. Smile when appropriate, and if you're introverted like me, then try to remember to smile at least three to four times during the interview, especially when you first meet the interviewer.

- **Appearance**: As much as that person you follow on social media might want you to believe that appearance doesn't matter, it does. Be sure that you're well-groomed (and showered, please) and dress appropriately. I do recommend a suit (men and women) if you have one, but in most interviews, business casual is fine. I would suggest asking the person who set up the interview what the dress code is. With the global pandemic in recent years, many interviews have moved virtually through things such as **Zoom**. You want to maintain the same dress code for virtual interviews because you don't know when you may find yourself standing up during the interview and being caught just wearing your shorts—or worse.

- **Research the company**: Do your homework on the company—its mission, current/future project initiatives, financials, and so on. I'm always amazed at how many people show up to an interview without having done any **open source intelligence (OSINT)** on the company.

  Think of it this way—if some person you didn't know walked up to you and proposed marriage, would you say yes? Or would you say no because you hadn't vetted them at all? Be smart. Do your homework.

- **Don't bad-mouth a past employer or team**: Yes—some companies (and some people) suck, but no one wants a negative person on their team. I remember a person I worked with many years ago who was negative about everything, and several productive people left the team because they were tired of hearing the endless complaints.

  Remember—it only takes one bad apple on a team to change team dynamics and reduce the team's productivity.

- **Don't be emotional**: Remember—this is business, so don't get emotional when talking about past companies, and so on. The interviewer is not your therapist.

- **Be concise in your answers**: For most people, this means you need to practice your answers to common interview questions and figure out how you can say less to get the same point across.

I find myself rambling, especially if I get on a live **question-and-answer (Q&A)** session with students because I am so excited to educate them.

Here are some of the things I used to do during a job interview to reduce my rambling:

- *To make a long story short* is a phrase I use if I think I'm rambling so that I can wrap up whatever I am saying. You have to practice this and be conscious of the fact you are rambling for this one to be effective.

- **Keep your answer short**. I used to answer interviewer questions with just a few words and then ask them if they wanted to know anything more about what I had mentioned.

Definition of cybersecurity

Now that you have some basic tips for your interview, let's talk about this whole cybersecurity thing in case you're new to the field.

If you ask 100 people the definition of cybersecurity, you'll get 100 different answers. Likewise, you'll notice I combine **cybersecurity** into a single word in this book, while others separate it as **cyber security**.

My favorite definition of cybersecurity comes from Dr. Mansur Hasib's best-selling book, *Cybersecurity Leadership*, as follows:

"Cybersecurity is the mission-focused and risk-optimized governance of information, which maximizes confidentiality, integrity, and availability using a balanced mix of people, policy, and technology, while perennially improving over time." (Hasib, 2015, p. 3)

In my opinion, understanding the definition of cybersecurity and how cybersecurity can be a business enabler that evolves over time can help you grow your cybersecurity career.

The HACK method

I could feel beads of sweat forming on my forehead as I stared at my computer screen in the darkness of the night. My stomach churned as I watched the timer count down and I thought *Will I make it in time?*

Was I doing some top-secret hack against an alien spaceship to save the world?

No—I had simply procrastinated in writing some papers for my classes, and I now had less than an hour to write three lengthy papers.

Besides, I didn't have my hoodie and gloves on, which we all know is a requirement of any successful hacker (just google it if you don't understand the joke here).

With a few minutes left, I submitted all three papers and received an excellent grade on all of them.

What was my secret? Did I hack into the professor's computer to change my grades? In hindsight, that might have been a good option, but instead, I had learned a long time ago how to hack myself.

In a similar fashion, you can learn to **hack** yourself for job interviews using the simple HACK method.

Have a look at the following definitions of the HACK method:

- **How**

  When applying for jobs, think about how your life is impacted by getting this job. Many people will just focus on the money here, but also ask yourself how this job fits into things such as your long-term plans. What sacrifices do you have to make (missing birthday parties, long commute to the office, and so on) for this job?

  Here are a few things I used to always think about:

  - *How long is the commute?* I once had to commute 4+ hours each way for a job, so I'd spend much of the week just sleeping in my car near the job site.

  - *How much earning ability do I have?* Is this just a base salary, or is there an option to earn more with stock options, sales commission, and so on?

  - *How much time will I really spend on this job?* Because most of us are paid for 40 hours a week in the US, but work 60+ hours each week.

  - *How does this job benefit my 1-, 5-, and 10-year goals?*

- **Analyze**

  The next part of HACK is analyzing yourself. There are a number of self-assessments out there on the internet, and all sorts of personality and aptitude assessments, and so on.

  Those are fine to take, but the low-cost route is to get a piece of paper (or your phone notes) and write down what you think is important, how you work through problems/projects, how good you are at time management, and so on.

  This is important, so be honest with yourself.

  As an example, I do the self-analysis monthly and I know that I am willing to go without eating, sleeping, and entertainment so that I can finish a project. I have no hesitation in sacrificing to complete the *mission*, which is how I was able to write those 20+-page papers in a short period of time. I also know that I can complete projects quickly, so I sometimes procrastinate until the deadline.

- **Collect**

  It's important to collect information about yourself on a continuous basis. The good news is, you'll likely secure that information better than the large companies out there.

  It's also important for you to collect information about the job you are applying for, the company itself (as mentioned earlier in this book), and what your long-term goals are.

- **Know**

  You need to know what success looks like for you. For example, one cybersecurity professional I know makes a lower salary but is able to get off at 5 p.m. every day to have dinner with the family. He's happy with his job, and that is success for him.

  Another cybersecurity professional I know is single and working at a major tech company working 80+ hour weeks but making close to a million in total compensation. This is the definition of success for her.

  It's crucial to know what success looks like for you and not what people on social media tell you success is.

  If you built a life that you never had to take a vacation from, what would that life look like?

Personal branding and soft skills

Many of the hiring managers I have spoken with over the years have mentioned that soft skills are a key part of the ideal candidate. In this section, we will discuss how personal branding and soft skills can help you achieve your goals. Your personal brand can help you develop more confidence, provide better job security, and increase your earnings over your career. When I developed my personal brand years ago, I went from living paycheck to paycheck to having financial freedom.

Personal branding

"Two all-beef patties, special sauce, lettuce, cheese, pickles, onions on a sesame seed bun" was a commercial jingle from McDonald's in the 1970s. I first heard it years later and I still remember it now.

That's the power of proper branding.

You are a brand, and you have value. Your personal brand brings value to any organization and helps them make more money.

Let me ask you a question. If you work hard for your brand and a company makes more money because of your brand, wouldn't it make sense for you to earn more money as well? Hopefully, you answered yes.

There are many books on personal branding and many ways to build your personal brand. I typically would tell you to focus on **LinkedIn** and show what you know through videos/screen recordings, posts, or articles/whitepapers.

Your personal brand can help you get jobs.

Imagine the *no spray and pray* resume and job application approach—no *we have a few more candidates to interview* type of stuff and no real pushback on the salary you want. All of this is made possible by your personal brand.

Soft skills

You might hear of many companies that advertise they need people with soft skills. Some of the key soft skills I think someone needs to have are the ability to communicate effectively across different stakeholders, the ability to work in a team, and customer service skills.

Negotiation 101

Everyone is in sales is a statement from one of my mentors many years ago.

Would you be opposed to me teaching you a trick I have used over the years to win at job interviews and—especially—negotiations?

Most people would answer *no* to that question because it's easier for most people to answer with a *no* to a question.

I won't deep dive into sales techniques in this book, but a good sales book is *The Sandler Rules* by David Mattson, and a guy named Josh Braun also has some good training.

Here are a few questions I have used over the years in interviews:

- **Would you be opposed to…?**

  Here's an example:

  Would you be opposed to me asking about career advancement for this job role?

- **Would it make sense…?**

  Here's an example:

  Would it make sense for us to discuss salary after we've seen this is a good match?

- **Can you offer your advice on…?**

    Here's an example:

    Can you offer your advice on how the team manages projects?

- **It seems…?**

    (Note: shut up after you use this one and let them respond)

    Here's an example:

    It seems like you need a minimum salary expectation to move me forward in the application process.

Managing stress

Years ago, I read a book called *How to Stop Worrying and Start Living* by Dale Carnegie. I'm not going to share everything in that book (you should buy a copy), but one key exercise had you reflecting on the worst possible scenario that could happen and then asking yourself if you were OK with that happening. If your answer was no, then you had to think through what action you could take to improve the situation.

Here's an example:

- **Scenario**: Your boss wants a project done by Monday, even though the real deadline is 3 weeks away.

- **Worst-case scenario**: You don't do the project on your days off, and the boss fires you because of it.

Are you OK with this?

Yes, because you already have money saved up to cover expenses while you look for another job. This gives you some freedom, and typically, this scenario wouldn't lead to termination since the project is not due for weeks.

No—you really need this job to pay your bills. In this situation, you probably have to suck it up this time and get the project done. However, I would suggest you then focus your spare time on building additional income streams, saving more money, and/or finding a new job. Otherwise, the cycle will just repeat itself.

I read another book years ago (can't think of the name) that mentioned reading just 6 minutes a day could reduce your stress by around 30 percent. I've found that reading can help take your mind away from stressful situations.

Another good book on the subject is *Chaos Loves You: So Let's Love it Back* by Jothi Dugar (cybersecurity executive).

I also practice simple meditation and breathing exercises.

Going back to what I mentioned earlier in the book as well, how you talk to yourself is crucial in your success and in removing stress from your life.

I'm not going to lie to you—cybersecurity careers can be extremely stressful. It's important for you to recognize if you're stressed out and identify safe ways to cope. Remember, we as a community are here to support you.

Now that you have a good idea of some common interview questions you might be asked, the questions you should ask, the HACK method, and a few books I suggest you buy around stress management, let's move into job-specific interview questions in the coming chapters.

Summary

In this chapter, you learned about common interview questions asked in many job interviews. Studying these questions and writing down your answers to them in advance of a job interview can help the interview be less stressful. Speaking of stress, you also learned a simple method for analyzing a situation to help lower your stress level about the situation. You also learned how to *hack* yourself for job interviews. Understanding yourself and your situation (situational awareness) is critical to your success in job interviews and in life.

In the next chapter, you will learn about SOC analyst careers and some common knowledge questions you might be asked in a job interview.

Part 2: Cybersecurity Careers and Interview Questions

This part will cover a brief overview of different hands-on technical cybersecurity careers, along with average salary ranges in the United States and common interview questions relating to such careers.

This part of the book comprises the following chapters:

2
SOC Analyst

In this chapter, you will learn what a **security operations center** (**SOC**) analyst is and the average salary range for this career in the United States. You will also learn about the career progression options and learn common interview questions for the role.

The following topics will be covered in this chapter:

- What is a SOC analyst?
- How much can you make in this career?
- What other careers can you do?
- Common interview questions for a SOC analyst career

What is a SOC analyst?

SOC analysts work as members of a managed security services team. There are typically three tiers of SOC analysts, and job-specific duties may vary based on the organization you work for:

- **SOC level 1 (tier 1) analysts** typically monitor security tools, such as **endpoint detection and response (EDR)** and **security information and event management (SIEM)** tools, to identify potential anomalous activity on networks and systems. If anomalous activity is detected, they then escalate it to level 2 analysts.

- **SOC level 2 (tier 2) analysts** investigate anomalous behavior. In some instances, they may perform **incident response (IR)** duties and initial malware analysis. You might build IR playbooks and perform scripting to automate routine tasks. You might also see level 2 skills being requested for incident responder job postings. Your tier 2 SOC analyst might also set up the access for jump boxes and do light forensic investigation work.

- **SOC level 3 (tier 3) analysts** perform IR and also typically perform threat hunting and threat profiling. They may also do some work in reverse engineering malware and digital forensics depending on their organization. You might see these job openings listed as incident responders or threat analysts/hunters. One thing to keep in mind if you are transitioning from another career to cybersecurity is you can often find non-traditional jobs at a cybersecurity product company and use this as the starting point for your career. As an example, if you are transitioning from selling used cars, you could get a job with the sales team at a security company such as Splunk. The company will then train you on all of their cybersecurity product and service offerings for free, then in 6 to 12 months, you will have a better chance of getting a cybersecurity job because you will then have experience at Splunk and you have experience with their different product offerings so you have in-demand skills. Many people focus on getting jobs as a SOC analyst or penetration tester because that's what their guidance counselor tells them to do, but it is often a better idea to look at non-traditional jobs to get your start in a cybersecurity career because others are not applying for those jobs. If you look at the Splunk company website, you will see hundreds of open non-traditional jobs, at the time of writing, that can be leveraged to get your start in a rewarding cybersecurity career.

How much can you make in this career?

SOC analyst salaries can vary significantly by location, company, and other factors. In the United States, you can expect to make between $60,000 and $85,000 for an entry-level SOC level 1 role.

What other careers can you do?

A career as a SOC analyst builds a solid foundational skill set and can help you prepare for many cybersecurity careers. Some examples are a forensic investigator, reverse engineer, penetration tester, GRC analyst, and CISO.

Common interview questions for a SOC analyst career

In the following sections, you will learn about common interview questions, including general knowledge, attack types, and tools, that you might experience in interviews for a SOC analyst position. The questions are listed with answers. A key item to note is that you want to keep your answers as short as possible during the interview and then just ask the interviewer whether they need you to expand upon the subject.

Remember that *clear and concise make the interview nice.*

General SOC knowledge questions

In this section, you will see some general SOC knowledge questions that might be asked in a SOC analyst interview:

- **What is information security and how is it achieved?**

  Information security just means protecting the confidentiality, integrity, and availability of information. It is achieved through risk management, where you identify the valuable information, identify any assets related to that information, identify vulnerabilities, identify threats to the CIA of the information, and identify the impact to the information and the organization if an incident occurs.

- **Explain risk, vulnerability, and threat.**

  Vulnerability is a weakness in a system. Vulnerabilities are weaknesses. This means there is a gap in the protection of a system. A **threat** is an attacker that is trying to exploit the vulnerability for their own gain.

Risk is the measure of potential loss when the vulnerability is exploited by the threat actor.

If you think of a house, a vulnerability (weakness) might be not paying the bill for your alarm monitoring company. A threat actor (burglar in this case) might use this weakness to get into your house. You would need to analyze the risk to see whether you have valuables inside of your home that justify the cost of paying for the alarm monitoring service.

- **What is the difference between asymmetric and symmetric encryption, and which one is better?**

Symmetric encryption uses the same key to encrypt and decrypt. Asymmetric encryption uses different keys to encrypt and decrypt.

Both have benefits and drawbacks. Symmetric encryption is normally faster than asymmetric, but the key needs to be transferred over an unencrypted channel. Asymmetric is slower but more secure. It's best to use a hybrid of the two.

- **What is an IPS and how does it differ from an IDS?**

An **intrusion detection system** (**IDS**) detects an intrusion and then will just alert the administrator for them to take further action.

An **intrusion protection system** (**IPS**) will detect the intrusion and then take action to prevent the intrusion.

- **What is the difference between encryption and hashing?**

Encryption is reversible and hashing is one-way. Hashing can be cracked in some cases using rainbow tables and collision attacks, but it is not reversible. Hashing ensures the integrity of data, and encryption ensures the confidentiality of data. A simple way to remember the difference between the two is that hashing protects the integrity of data and is one-way, and encryption is used to protect the data itself and is two-way, meaning once you encrypt something, you can then decrypt it to see the data in its original form.

- **What is a security misconfiguration?**

A security misconfiguration is where the network, application, or device, for example, is configured to allow an attacker to exploit it easily. One of the most common security misconfigurations in both the consumer and B2B space is the use of default login credentials. Another common security misconfiguration involves cloud environments, where access to sensitive data is not restricted.

- **What are black hat, white hat, and gray hat hackers?**

Black hat is used to describe someone who does not have the authorization to access systems or data but attempts to do so anyway. A white hat (ethical) hacker has permission from the owner. A gray hat hacker hacks without permission but does it for the greater good. A good example of a gray hat was the hacker that hacked home **wireless access points (WAPs)** to update the firmware, so users would be protected against a critical vulnerability (`https://www.zdnet.com/article/a-mysterious-grey-hat-is-patching-peoples-outdated-mikrotik-routers/`).

- **What is a firewall?**

A firewall is like a gate guard. Based on a set of predefined rules, it either allows traffic or not, similar to a gate guard allowing you to go through the gate and visit Oprah or not.

In modern networks, firewalls are still used but there is really no *perimeter* anymore due to things such as **bring your own device (BYOD)**.

- **How do you keep yourself updated with the information security news?**

This question helps the interviewer understand your passion and motivation for the role. You can use something such as **Feedly** to aggregate cybersecurity news into a single location for review or just follow some of the more common sources of news (such as Threatpost, The CyberWire, and The Hacker News). No one expects you to know everything that is going on, but you should have a good idea of the major news each week in the cyber world.

- **The world has recently been hit by an attack (that is, SolarWinds). What would you do to protect your organization as a security professional?**

If you have some experience, you can answer this using that as an example. If this is your first cyber role, then focus on the IR steps listed in *NIST SP 800-61*.

- **What is the CIA triad?**

  The CIA triad can be defined as follows:

  - **Confidentiality** is just making sure that only the right people, systems, or applications can access data. Think of confidentiality as locking your data in a safe, and only giving access to people you trust.

  - **Integrity** is making sure the data has not been altered.

  - **Availability** is making sure the right users can access the right information when they need to. In some industries, such as critical infrastructure, availability comes before confidentiality and integrity on the priority list.

- **HIDS and NIDS – which one is better and why?**

  A **host intrusion detection system (HIDS)** is just an IDS that lives on a host machine. A drawback of host-based detection is it can consume a lot more processing power than a **network intrusion detection system (NIDS)**. Both HIDSs and NIDSs perform similar actions, but an HIDS offers more visibility into suspicious activity on the endpoint.

- **What is a security policy?**

  A security policy is a document that outlines how to protect an organization from threats, and the procedures for responding to incidents.

- **What are the core principles of information security?**

  The core principles are as follows:

  - Confidentiality

  - Integrity

  - Availability

- **What is non-repudiation (as it applies to IT security)?**

  Non-repudiation basically means that neither the sender nor receiver of the information can deny that they processed the information. The sender or receiver could be human-to-human communication, human-to-machine, or machine-to-machine.

- **What is the relationship between information security and data availability?**

  Information security entails protecting data and ensuring that only authorized entities can access the data. Data availability just means that the authorized entities can access the data when they need to.

- **What is the difference between logical and physical security? Can you give an example of both?**

  Physical security is preventing unauthorized entities from physically accessing things they should not have access to. For example, you put up a fence around your house, set up CCTV cameras, get an alarm system, and get a dog. These are all examples of physical security controls to stop unauthorized access.

  Logical security covers the electronic form of preventing unauthorized access. You might do this through something such as using encryption for data in transit and rest so no one else can read the data.

- **What's an acceptable level of risk?**

  This depends on the risk appetite of the organization.

- **Can you give me an example of common security vulnerabilities?**

  For this question, I would keep it simple and focus on a few things such as security misconfigurations, **identity and access management (IAM)** of third parties, and credential reuse. You can then ask the interviewer whether they need you to expand on anything else.

- **Are you familiar with any security management frameworks, such as ISO/IEC 27002?**

  If you didn't know what this is, look it up. *ISO 27002* is just a framework of security controls organizations can use to help improve their security posture. You should have at least a high-level understanding of popular security control frameworks.

- **What is a security control?**

  Security controls are safeguards, parameters, and countermeasures used to protect data, services, and business operations.

- **What are the different types of security controls?**

  There are three main types of security controls:

  - **Technical controls** are also known as **logical controls**. Examples of technical controls include things such as using encryption, ACLs, firewalls, IDS/IPS, SIEM tools, and anti-virus software.

  - **Administrative controls** are policies, procedures, or guidelines that help the organization manage its risk. The implementation of administrative controls is executed by people and is called the **operational controls**.

  - **Physical security controls** include things such as CCTV cameras, alarm systems, security guards, ID scanners, locks, and biometrics.

- **What is information security governance?**

  Information security governance is the accountability framework for security in an organization. In many cases, C-level executives will set the risk appetite for the organization and define compliance and performance objectives. A cybersecurity manager will then identify how to implement security and set risk tolerance so that the organization does not exceed the risk appetite.

- **Are open source projects more or less secure than proprietary ones?**

  This depends on the size of the project, the background of the developers, and the quality controls in place. Many hiring managers are looking for you to list out a few pros and cons for both of them. This shows them you are able to think through projects that might use one or the other.

- **Who do you look up to within the field of information security? Why?**

  Hopefully, you answer *Ken Underhill* for this one, but even if you don't, just know that this question is being asked to see whether you are willing to accept mentorship from more experienced professionals. If you don't have any senior cybersecurity professionals you follow on social media, it could indicate to the hiring manager that you are not that interested in cybersecurity or that you are against taking advice from other team members.

- **How would you find out what a POST code means?**

  Power on self test (POST) is a diagnostic check your computer runs during the boot process. Unless you have the beep codes memorized, the answer to this question is simply *I would search online*.

  Some of the POST (beep) codes are as follows:

  - **One beep**: This is a refresh failure, so you might need to check your memory card or the motherboard.

  - **Two beeps**: This is a parity error.

  - **Three beeps**: This is a memory error.

  - **Four beeps**: This is a timer failure.

  - **Five beeps**: This is a processor failure.

  - **Six beeps**: This is a keyboard controller failure.

  - **Seven beeps**: This is a virtual mode exception error.

  - **Eight beeps**: This is a display memory failure.

- **What is the chain of custody?**

  The chain of custody is essentially the paper trail showing who has handled evidence from the time the evidence was collected until the time it is presented in a court of law.

- **Do you prefer filtered ports or closed ports on your firewall?**

  My answer for this one would be closed ports. By closing ports, I limit the attack surface.

- **What is a honeypot?**

  At a high level, a honeypot is designed to attract adversaries so you can see how they are attacking systems. This can help your detection capabilities by helping you understand what actions the threat actor needs to take at each stage of the Cyber Kill Chain for the adversary to be successful in their attack. You can then build detection for those actions and stop attacks.

- **What information security challenges are faced in a cloud computing environment?**

  There are many challenges. A few you should answer with are IAM, security misconfigurations, visibility into your cloud infrastructure and assets, and insider threats.

- **How many bits do you need for an IPv4 subnet mask?**

  Subnet masks are 32 bits for IPv4.

- **What are the layers of the OSI model?**

  I've listed the layers in the list that follows, but you will also want to understand how data flows through these layers and understand what the term *encapsulation* means. I've listed encapsulation as the next question, but typically they (OSI and then encapsulation) will be asked about concurrently in a real job interview:

  - **Layer 1** – The physical layer, which is where raw bitstream is transferred over a physical medium (that is, fiber optic cable, copper cables, and electromagnetic waves).

  - **Layer 2** – The data link layer that controls the transfer of data between nodes on the same LAN segment and contains the sub-layers of **media access control (MAC)** and **logical link control (LLC)**. This layer is where you see the MAC address (example – `ff:ff:ff:ff:ff:ff`) and the information at this layer is labeled as `frames`.

- **Layer 3** – The network layer, which decides what path the data will take. This layer transports and routes the packets across network boundaries. Information at this layer is labeled as a packet and this is where IP routing lives. An example of an **Internet Protocol version 4 (IPv4)** address at this layer would be 192.168.0.55 and an example of an **Internet Protocol version 6 (IPv6)** address at this layer would be 2001:0DB6:A C10:FE01:0000:0000:0000:0000 or written in the shorter version 2001:0DB6:AC10:FE01::::. Some of the protocols at this layer are **Address Resolution Protocol (ARP)**, **Reverse Address Resolution Protocol (RARP)**, **Domain Name System (DNS)**, **Internet Control Message Protocol (ICMP)**, And **Dynamic Host Configuration Protocol (DHCP)**.

- **Layer 4** – The transport layer, which transmits the data using protocols such as **Transmission Control Protocol (TCP)** And **User Datagram Protocol (UDP)**. The transport layer is responsible for segmenting the data from applications into a manageable size and the information is labeled as a segment at this layer. The UDP protocol is faster than TCP but it just sends the data and doesn't care whether the data was received on the other end. With TCP, a three-way handshake is established, which allows the sender to know the data was received by the intended recipient.

- **Layer 5** – The session layer, which maintains connections and controls the ports and sessions. The session layer handles the creation, use, and break down of a session. It also handles token management for the session.

- **Layer 6** – The presentation layer, which is where data is presented in a usable format and also where data is encrypted. This layer preserves the syntax of the data that is being transmitted and also handles compression and decompression of the data.

- **Layer 7** – The application layer, where interaction with applications occurs. Some examples of the protocols at layer 7 are **Hypertext Transfer Protocol (HTTP)**, **Secure Shell (SSH)**, **File Transport Protocol (FTP)**, And **Simple Mail Transfer Protocol (SMTP)**.

- **What is encapsulation?**

  As data moves through the layers of the OSI model, each layer encapsulates the data by adding a header and sometimes a trailer to the data.

> **Note**
>
> One thing I've noticed before in interviews is that the hiring managers mistakenly think data encapsulation is just encryption of the data. Yes, encryption of the data can occur at the presentation layer, but it doesn't always happen. This goes to show you that *experienced* professionals can still make mistakes on the fundamentals.

- **What are the three ways to authenticate a person?**

  They are as follows:

  - Using something you know, such as your password
  - Using something you have, such as a smart ID card
  - Using something you are, such as a fingerprint

- **What is worse in firewall detection, a false negative or a false positive? And why?**

  A false negative is worse because you don't know that an attack has occurred.

- **What is the primary reason most companies haven't fixed their vulnerabilities?**

  Contrary to what media outlets claim, there could be a number of reasons why a company hasn't fixed vulnerabilities. I would just list out a few and then ask the interviewer whether they want you to go into more detail.

  Many media outlets will state the cost of fixing vulnerabilities is more than the cost of a data breach to the company. This is correct in many cases.

  Another reason might be the company is running legacy applications that don't allow them to update to the latest OS version. I ran into this a few years ago at a healthcare company that was still running the Windows 2000 server.

  There's also the issue of unpatchable vulnerabilities and vulnerabilities that are not a significant risk to the organization.

- **What is the three-way handshake? How can it be used to create a DOS attack?**

  The TCP three-way handshake is a way to establish communication between a client and server. A SYN packet is sent from the client to the server. The server acknowledges the communication (ACK) and also sends back its own SYN packet. The client then confirms receipt with an **ACK** packet.

  That's the simple definition. Some interviewers may want you to go deeper into this where you discuss sequencing.

An attacker can use this for a **denial-of-service (DoS)** attack by simply sending a SYN packet to the server. The server will then respond with a SYN/ACK and be waiting for an ACK response from the attacker. Instead, the attacker keeps sending SYN packets and the server's bandwidth is eaten up by its responses to the SYN packets.

- **What are some of the responsibilities of level 1 and 2 SOC analysts?**

  This question helps the interviewer understand how much you know about the role and its common responsibilities.

  Some responsibilities of a level 1 (tier 1) SOC analyst include monitoring for malicious and anomalous behavior in network and system traffic through tools such as SIEMs and IDSs, using ticketing systems, and escalating suspicious activity found to level 2 analysts for review.

  Level 2 (tier 2) SOC analysts perform triaging of alerts using playbooks. Level 2 analysts may also tune the collection tools to help reduce false positives and use the MITRE ATT&CK framework (https://attack.mitre.org/) to identify security gaps in the organization's defensive posture. At this level, you will also remove malware from end user systems and write YARA rules to detect and stop future attacks.

- **What are the steps to building a SOC?**

  This is normally a question asked as a more senior level 2 or 3 SOC analyst. A goal here is to see how you would use your knowledge and experience to architect a SOC from the ground up. The steps to building a SOC include the following:

  1. Develop your SOC strategy: The key to developing your strategy is to understand the current state of your organization and perform the following:

  - Assess your existing capabilities.
  - Delay non-core functions until your core functions are sufficiently mature.
  - Identify and define business objectives from stakeholders.

  2. Design your SOC solution:

  - Choose a few business-critical use cases (for example, a phishing attack).
  - Define your initial solution based on these use cases.
  - Consider that your solution must be able to meet the future needs of the organization.

Remember, a narrow scope will help reduce the time to initial implementation, which will help you achieve results faster.

3. Create processes, procedures, and training:

- Identify and analyze threats to determine the nature and extent of risk to the organization.
- Implement countermeasures to mitigate threat actors and the associated risk.

4. Prepare your environment before deploying the SOC:

- Ensure SOC staff desktops, laptops, and mobile devices are secured.
- Limit remote access for SOC staff (and third parties if applicable).
- Require MFA for all accounts.

5. Implement your solution and leverage technology where applicable:

- Deploy your log management infrastructure.
- Onboard your minimum collection of critical data sources.
- Deploy your security analytics capabilities.
- Deploy your **Security orchestration, automation and response (SOAR)** solution.
- Begin deploying use cases to focus on end-to-end threat detection and response.
- Incorporate threat intelligence feeds.
- Employ detection engineering.
- Incorporate automation.

6. Implement and test your use cases:

- Test your use cases.
- Analyze the security and reliability of your security solution.

7. Maintain and improve your SOC:

- Tune to improve detection accuracy.
- Add other systems as inputs or outputs.
- Review the SOC, SOC roles, and staff counts.

- **What is data protection in transit versus data protection at rest?**

The protection for the data in both of these scenarios is to encrypt the data. As the name implies, data protection in transit just means you are protecting the data from end to end while it's being transmitted. Data at rest just means the data is protected while it is being stored.

- **Is it an issue to give all users administrator-level access?**

Yes, this is an issue, and you will want to implement the principle of least privilege as part of IAM.

- **How do you protect your home WAP?**

Turn off broadcasting of your SSID, update the firmware, change the default credentials, and use strong and unique passwords and MFA.

- **How can you tell whether a remote server is running IIS or Apache?**

You can run a simple scan with a tool such as *Nmap* to see what it is running and the version. You could also do banner grabbing.

- **How often should you perform patch management?**

This depends on a number of factors. Some patches might need to be applied immediately, while you might cycle others on a specific date. Microsoft has its famous Patch Tuesday, but not all organizations implement patches on this day. It's usually best to test patches on non-production systems and networks, so you can identify whether the patch is breaking anything else.

- **What is Docker?**

Docker uses OS-level virtualization and delivers infrastructure as code through containers. What does this mean? It means you can run a virtualized infrastructure at low or no cost on just about any computer you have. What does this mean for a company? It usually means significant infrastructure savings.

- **Are VXLANs scalable?**

Yes, VXLANs are used for their scalability in comparison to using a traditional VLAN for network segmentation.

- **What is the difference between TCP and UDP?**

TCP is connection-orientated and UDP is a connectionless protocol. This means TCP will attempt to establish the three-way handshake. UDP is usually faster than TCP communication.

- **What is a playbook/runbook in SOC?**

  A playbook, also known as a **standard operating procedure** (**SOP**), consists of a set of guidelines to handle security incidents and alerts in the SOC. For example, if credentials were compromised, the playbook would help the level 1 SOC analyst know what actions they should take.

- **What is the difference between firewall deny and drop?**

  If the firewall is set to a **deny rule**, it will block the connection and send a reset packet back to the sender. This alerts the sender that there is a firewall being used.

  If the firewall is set to a **drop rule**, it will block the connection request without notifying the sender. It is recommended that you configure the firewall to deny egress (outbound) traffic and set the incoming traffic to just drop, so an attacker doesn't know you are filtering the traffic with a firewall.

- **Explain the different SOC models.**

  There are three types of models in SOC:

  - An in-house model, where all the resources, technology, processes, and SOC employee training are managed within the organization.

  - A **managed security service provider** (**MSSP**), where a third-party security service provider manages all of the resources, technology, processes, and training of SOC staff.

  - A hybrid SOC model, where level 1 is outsourced to an MSSP and then the organization has level 2 and above in-house. Many large companies use this model.

- **What is DNS?**

  DNS is basically the phone book (I might be giving my age away with this example) of the internet. As an example, let's say that you type `google.com` in your browser and the domain name (`google.com`) is then translated to an IP address (`192.168.0.1` for this example) for Google's servers so you can see the information on their website. This eliminates the need for you to memorize every server IP address of Google.

There are four DNS servers involved in your request to access Google's web page:

- The **DNS recursor** receives queries from clients and then makes any additional requests to satisfy the client's DNS query. This is similar to you requesting a book from the library and the librarian looking up the shelf that the book is on and then handing the book to you.

- The **root nameserver** is the first step in translating human-readable information (that is, google.com) into an IP address. Using our library analogy, this is like the index card that tells you the book is in the non-fiction section. Using our google.com example, this nameserver would tell you that the web page you want is in the *Google* section of the library.

- The **top-level domain** (**TLD**) nameserver is the next step and hosts the last portion of the hostname (.com in our google.com example). In our library example, this would be the librarian telling you that the book is on shelf 12 of the *Google* section.

- The **authoritative** nameserver can be thought of as the master index card that tells you specifically where the book is in the library.

One thing to keep in mind is that DNS uses multiple servers and not a single server.

- **You receive an email from your bank stating that there is a problem with your account. The email states you need to log in to your account to verify your identity and even provides a link to your bank. If you don't verify your identity, the email states that your account will be frozen. Tomorrow is payday and you need to pay your rent that is past due via a wire transfer in the morning. What should you do?**

This is a simple phishing attack, and the question is designed to test your general knowledge of phishing since you might have end users calling the SOC with this issue. In this example, you should not click any links or documents in that email. Instead, visit the bank's website URL directly or call your bank. You should also change the password for your bank account. Most banks don't typically contact you via email if there is an issue with your account.

After answering this question, you can ask the interviewer whether they need you to explain what phishing is.

- **A friend of yours sends you an e-card via email. To view the e-card, you have to click on an attachment. What do you do?**

The answer is you don't click anything. Your friend's email address could have been spoofed and/or the attachment could be infected, and your friend simply didn't realize that before sending it to you.

- **You are a new level 1 SOC analyst and receive a call from the IT helpdesk to ensure you can access all systems. The IT helpdesk person is friendly to you and asks you to confirm your password, so they can verify you meet the minimum complexity requirements. What do you do?**

  This is a **vishing (phishing via phone)** attack. One part of this answer is to hang up the phone, but before you do, I would try to get as much information as possible from the individual. I've had this happen before and I was able to get a postal mailing address (I told them I wanted to personally mail them a thank you card for being so helpful) out of the individual. The mailing address turned out to be a mailbox at a UPS store, but it was an additional clue for law enforcement to hopefully catch the criminal calling me.

- **What is cognitive cybersecurity?**

  Cognitive cybersecurity is the application of **artificial intelligence (AI)**, patterned on human thought processes, to detect threats and protect physical and digital systems. It uses data mining, pattern recognition, and natural language processing to simulate the human brain.

- **What is the difference between SIEM and IDS systems?**

  SIEM and IDS systems collect log data.

  SIEM tools facilitate event correlation to identify patterns that might indicate an attack has occurred, and centralize log data.

  IDS tools also capture log data but do not facilitate event correlation. The purpose of an IDS is to detect an intrusion and alert on the intrusion.

- **What is port blocking?**

  The answer is simply blocking ports. It's helpful to block unnecessary ports so you can reduce the attack surface. One thing to keep in mind though is that many threat actors just use ports they know will always be open (HTTPS on port 443 as an example).

- **What is ARP and how does it work?**

  Address Resolution Protocol (ARP) is a protocol for mapping an **Internet Protocol address (IP address)** to a physical machine address that is recognized in the local network.

How does it work?

I.   When an incoming packet is destined for a host machine on the LAN at the gateway, the gateway asks the ARP program to find the physical host or MAC address that matches the IP address.

II.   The ARP program looks in the ARP cache and, if it finds the address, provides it so that the packet can be converted to the right packet length and format and sent to the host machine.

III. If no entry is found for the IP address, ARP broadcasts a request packet in a special format to all the machines on the LAN to see whether one machine knows that it has that IP address associated with it.

- **What is port scanning?**

Port scanning is a technique used to identify open ports and services available on a host. A threat actor can use port scanning to identify services running and identify vulnerabilities that can be exploited. A network administrator might use port scanning to verify the security policies set on the network. **Nmap** is a popular tool that can be used for port scanning.

- **A senior executive approaches you and demands that you break security policy to let her access a social media website. What do you do?**

In this situation, I would ask why they need the access and then explain that it is against the security policy. If the executive persists, I would suggest getting your leadership team involved. Many companies have a formal process for one-off requests like this to be reviewed and approved.

- **Why would an organization bring in an outside consulting firm to perform a penetration test?**

A couple of reasons are as follows:

- It might be a requirement for compliance.

- You can tap into the broad skill set and expertise of the consulting firm without needing a full internal pen-testing team.

- **What is an insider threat?**

Insider threats are security risks that originate within the organization. They are anyone that has access to the organization's infrastructure or insider knowledge and/or access to sensitive data for the organization. Insider threats could be a third-party contractor, an executive, or a janitor. This is why they are difficult to protect against.

Not every insider threat is malicious in nature. You typically have two main types of insider threats:

- **Turncloaks** are the ones you likely think of, and they are the ones stealing data or performing malicious actions to harm the organization.

- **Pawns** are your everyday employees who are exploited by a threat actor or who make a mistake. Some examples include an employee who leaves their work laptop at the local coffee shop, which leads to data theft, and an employee falling for a vishing attack, where they reveal their login credentials to the *IT helpdesk* person on the phone.

The 2019 Verizon **Data Breach Investigation Report** (**DBIR**) showed over 30 percent of data breaches were the result of an insider threat.

It's also good in a job interview to cite some stats from the DBIR or the Ponemon Cost of a Data Breach Report. These show the interviewer that you are aware of industry reporting and trends.

- **What is a residual risk?**

Residual risk is the risk that remains after you implement security controls.

- **What is data loss prevention (DLP)?**

DLP tools are used to make sure that users are not sending sensitive data outside of the internal network.

Best practices for DLP include identifying data, classifying it, prioritizing it, understanding the risks to the data, monitoring data in transit, and creating controls to protect the data. You will also want to train your employees because many will not understand how their actions can result in data loss.

- **What is an incident response plan?**

IR plans ensure that the right people and procedures are in place to deal with threats. This allows your IR team to perform a structured investigation into events to determine the **indicator of compromise** (**IOC**) and the **tactics, techniques, and procedures** (**TTPs**) of the threat actor(s). An IR plan is like a step-by-step guide to follow if an incident occurs; however, you might jump around through different phases of the Kill Chain depending on the incident.

NIST 800-61 is a good resource for you to learn about the different phases of incident handling and you will likely be asked some questions on 800-61 for job interviews.

I've listed the phases as follows:

- Preparation

- Detection and analysis

- Containment, eradication, and recovery

- Post-incident activity

General attack knowledge questions

In this section, you will see some of the attack knowledge questions that might be asked in a SOC analyst interview:

- **What is a botnet?**

  A botnet is composed of hijacked computers that are used to perform a number of tasks, including attacks such as a DDoS. Some notable botnet infrastructures are Mirai, which hijacked IoT devices, and Emotet.

- **What are the most common types of attacks that threaten enterprise data security?**

  The answer to this will change as time progresses and new threats emerge but in general, it includes things such as malware/ransomware, DDoS/DoS attacks, phishing/**business email compromise (BEC)**, credential stuffing, and web application attacks.

- **What is XSS and how can you mitigate it?**

  Cross-site scripting (XSS) is a JavaScript vulnerability in different web applications. There are different types of XSS, including reflected and stored XSS. For reflected XSS, a user enters a script on the client side and this input gets processed without getting validated. This means the untrusted input is executed on the client side, typically through the browser.

  For stored XSS, a malicious script is injected directly into a vulnerable web application and executed. This means any user visiting the web app server will be infected, even if they clear their browser cache.

- **What is CSRF?**

  Cross-site request forgery (CSRF) is a vulnerability in web applications where the server does not validate the request as being from a trusted client. In layperson terms, let's say you are authenticated and logged into your banking website. If the bank's site doesn't have CSRF protection, an attacker could take over your session and send requests to the bank, such as transferring the money from your account to their account.

SOC tool questions

In this section, you will see questions on common SOC tools. Please note that this list will not contain every tool and that it's more important for you to understand what the different types of tools used in a SOC are versus knowing how to use every vendor tool. It's also important to note that the answers to these questions may change as tools are updated with new features:

- **What is Splunk?**

  Splunk is a SIEM tool that is used for searching, visualizing, monitoring, and reporting data. It offers real-time insight into your data. A key thing to remember for any tool question is you should know what that type of tool does at a high level. Splunk is just one brand of tool, so it's more important for you to understand what a SIEM tool is and what it does.

- **Why is Splunk used for analyzing data?**

  It offers business insights, which means it understands patterns hidden within data and turns them into real-time business insights that can be used to make informed business decisions. This is key because there is so much data to sift through in a typical enterprise and it's important to gain actionable insights into the data. It also provides visibility into your operations and proactive monitoring.

  Your answer here should be clear and concise on a few of the value props of Splunk or another SIEM tool. You can always ask the interviewer whether they would like you to provide more context or information.

- **What do SOAR solutions provide that SIEM tools usually don't?**

  SOAR tools provide orchestration, automation, responses, and collaboration. They also allow the company to integrate multiple resources into a single location. Many larger companies build their own custom SOAR tools that are optimized for their environment.

- **Which of the following use a user's behavior as part of their process to determine anomalous behavior on a network?**

  - EDR tools

  - SIEM tools

  - SOAR tools

  - UEBA tools

  The answer is UEBA tools. **UEBA** stands for **user and entity behavior analytics**. These tools are used to detect attacks faster by aggregating data from on-premises and the cloud and from multiple devices to detect anomalous behavior on the network that might be seen when an attacker moves into lateral movement.

- **Which components listed are seen with many next-gen SIEM solutions, but not traditional SIEMs?**

  - Threat intelligence feed

  - EDR

  - SOAR

  - UEBA

  UEBA and SOAR are often seen in next-generation SIEM solutions.

- **Select all of the SIEM tools from the following:**

  - Splunk

  - QRadar

  - Cisco ASA

  - Microsoft Sentinel

  The only one listed that is not a SIEM tool is Cisco ASA, which is a firewall.

As you can see, many interview questions as a SOC analyst are around attack types and fundamental knowledge of SIEM tools. The good news is that many companies are only looking for you to have knowledge of attacks and how threat actors might attack the organization as a tier 1 SOC analyst (entry level). I would also suggest you explore the MITRE ATT&CK framework to think through how organizations can use it operationally to build detection logic in their SIEM tool and how it can be used strategically by the organization to identify gaps in their security posture.

Summary

In this chapter, you learned about the SOC analyst career and the average salary range in the United States. You also learned how this can be a stepping stone into other cybersecurity careers and you learned common interview questions asked for SOC analyst roles.

In the next chapter, you will learn about a career as a penetration tester, including common knowledge-based interview questions you might be asked.

3
Penetration Tester

In this chapter, you will learn what a **penetration tester** (**pentester**) is and the average salary range for this career in the **United States** (**US**). You will also learn about career progression options and learn common interview questions for the role.

The following topics will be covered in this chapter:

- What is a pentester?
- How much can you make in this role?
- Which other roles can you do?
- Common interview questions for a pentester career

What is a pentester?

Penetration testing (**pentesting**) or ethical hacking is where you assess the security of networks, websites, endpoints, mobile devices, wireless devices, **operational technology/industrial control system** (**OT/ICS**) infrastructure, and the security of physical facilities. This assessment might include performing vulnerability scanning and analysis, reviewing source code, performing **open source intelligence** (**OSINT**), gaining access to a target by exploiting vulnerabilities, escalating privileges, maintaining persistence, and more.

A key thing here is that you have permission as a pentester to attack the target as defined in the **statement of work (SOW)** of the **penetration test (pentest)**. If you don't have permission, then it's illegal. Before starting action on any pentest, you need to review the **rules of engagement (ROEs)** and determine the scope of the pentest and verify that the client owns everything listed. I've reviewed SOWs before where the client mistyped an **Internet Protocol (IP)** address and we could have been in legal trouble for performing the pentest if we had not corrected the documentation. The right documentation is like a get-out-of-jail-free card during a pentest.

A goal of pentests is to simulate which vulnerabilities are exploitable by an adversary, and this is where vulnerability assessments and pentests differ. A vulnerability assessment just identifies that there might be something an adversary can exploit, and a pentest shows that it can be exploited and provides ways to mitigate the impact.

A good way to think of the difference between vulnerability assessments and pentesting is a car. Your mechanic runs a diagnostic scan (vulnerability assessment) on your car and identifies some error codes that tell the mechanic five problems that might be the cause. The mechanic then tinkers under the hood and manually assesses those potential problems (pentest), and ultimately determines the root cause. For example, you turn on the ignition on your car, but it just will not catch and actually start the car. This could be caused by the battery, ignition switch, spark plugs, or other parts. Your mechanic runs a diagnostic scan that will indicate all of these as potential issues and then checks each one to identify what the real problems are and provides recommendations to fix them (pentest).

There are many different areas of pentesting that you can specialize in, including applications (web apps, cloud, thick clients, mobile apps, and so on), infrastructure/networking, ICS, physical, red team, hardware, **Internet of Things (IoT)**, and social engineering. Many pentesters specialize in one or two of these areas and then also have knowledge and skills in other areas. No one is an expert in every area of pentesting, contrary to what you might see in the movies. Speaking of movies, real pentesting has nothing to do with wearing a hoodie in your mom's basement as binary code scrolls across the computer screen. Real-life pentesting takes careful planning and doesn't always involve you being an expert in computer programming, but it can be challenging and rewarding.

So, what skills do you need to be a pentester? For soft skills, passion and the ability to communicate the results of your pentest to stakeholders are critical. For technical skills, you need to have a solid foundation in operating systems, networking, and security.

The good news is that, as with most cybersecurity careers, you don't need a college degree or certifications to become a pentester.

If you are looking to gain hands-on experience with home labs, you can download VirtualBox (`https://www.virtualbox.org/`) or VMware Workstation (`https://www.vmware.com/products/workstation-player/workstation-player-evaluation.html`) for free and install Kali Linux (`https://www.kali.org/`) and Metasploitable (`https://sourceforge.net/projects/metasploitable/`) to practice. You can also find free Microsoft Windows (`https://www.microsoft.com/en-us/evalcenter/`) **International Organization for Standardization (ISO)** images here to build Windows **virtual machines (VMs)**.

Heath Adams who is a professional pentester also has free ethical hacking video training on YouTube. PortSwigger (`https://portswigger.net/web-security`) also has some free training for web application pentesting. If you just do a quick search online for *ethical hacking training* or *penetration testing training*, you should find hundreds of free and low-cost resources to help build your skills.

How much can you make in this role?

The salary range for a pentester in the US depends on a number of factors, such as your location, the size of the company you work for, certifications you hold, college degrees, and your skills. I've seen salaries as low as $76,000 and as high as $270,000+ for specialized public sector work. For a junior-level pentester, you can usually expect between $70,000 and $100,000, depending on the factors I mentioned before. I do want to mention that there are far more jobs available on the defensive side of the house versus the offensive.

Which other roles can you do?

A career as a pentester means you have mastered certain technical and soft skills, so it can help prepare you for any new roles in the industry. I've typically seen pentesters move into other types of pentesting (that is, application instead of infrastructure) or move into leadership roles in the C-suite.

Common interview questions for a pentester career

The questions that follow are primarily knowledge-based questions. During a junior pentester interview, you will likely experience many knowledge-based questions, with some hands-on testing assessments possible. For senior and principal pentester job interviews, you often receive a hands-on test of your pentesting skills after the initial phone screen from the recruiter or **human resources (HR)**. You're likely to encounter questions similar to these:

- **Where do you go to research the latest vulnerabilities, and why?**

  Your answer could include following specific security researchers on Twitter, following blogs such as Krebs and Threatpost, podcasts you listen to, and more. There isn't usually a wrong answer here, but the interviewer does want to see how you stay current on recent vulnerabilities and the latest cybersecurity news.

- **Do you have a favorite hacker in history, and why are they your favorite?**

  This question is asked to see how passionate you are about the history of hacking. This is another question with no wrong answer, and you might not have a favorite, which is OK. An example of a famous hacker in history is Kevin Mitnick.

- **What are some areas you are planning to improve in?**

  This question is being asked to see whether you are a continuous learner and to see how you identify areas of self-improvement. Even as a junior pentester, you should expect to be learning something new continuously, and you need to be able to assess your skill set and know the areas you need to improve in. For example, I'm good at social engineering but not so good at programming. As a pentester, I focused less practice on social engineering since that came naturally and focused instead on becoming better at coding so that I could write my own tools.

- **I need you to perform an internal pentest and I have an ROE document in place. What do you do next?**

  The interviewer is identifying your methodology for approaching a pentest with this question. If you're interviewing for your first pentesting job, you always want to make sure you review and verify the ROE (scoping) document to know what is off limits and what you can attack. Clients sometimes list wrong IP addresses, so you also need to verify that anything listed as available to attack is actually owned by the client. Otherwise, you can get yourself into legal trouble.

- **What are the types of cross-site scripting (XSS), and which is the most dangerous?**

  There are three types of XSS, which are reflected, stored, and **Document Object Model** (**DOM**)-based. The specific danger of each depends on the situation. Stored XSS is typically more dangerous because it is stored on the server side and the payload only has to be stored once to continue infecting anyone connecting to the server.

- **Can you explain XSS as though you were talking to a 10-year-old kid?**

  This question is designed to see whether you can break down complex cybersecurity topics for stakeholders. Here in the US, statistics vary, but most people understand it at an 8th-grade level or below, which means you have to communicate information to stakeholders as though they are 10-year-old kids in many situations. I would explain this one with something like this statement:

  With XSS, you can log in to anyone's account with a username and password. This is important to fix because an attacker can use attacks such as XSS to perform illegal transactions, which can lead to the company losing money.

  When you're presenting to corporate stakeholders, you can also mention how XSS can lead to cookie stealing and be used to perform privilege escalation and in phishing attacks.

- **How can you perform XSS if <script> or alert tags are blocked?**

  If `<script>` tags are blocked, you could use things such as image payloads or video payloads. Instead of using `alert` tags, you could use tags such as `prompt` and `confirm`.

- **What are some ways to mitigate XSS attacks?**

  You can use encoding, validate user input properly, sanitize output, and use **web application firewalls** (**WAFs**).

- **What was the last script that you wrote, and what was its purpose?**

  I want to stress here that as a junior pentester, you don't have to have coding skills, but if you want to be successful in the long term, it's important for you to learn at least one language so that you can write new tools on the fly during an engagement. This question is used to assess your scripting skills, and you might write something simple such as a keylogger that you can show off during the interview.

- **What are some types of threat actors?**

This question is usually looking for your broader knowledge of threat actors, so mentioning nation-state groups, state-sponsored groups, hacktivists, organized criminal gangs, script kiddies, and insider threats is good for this question. It's also a good idea to stay current on cybersecurity breaches and the threat actors behind them, or at least know a few of the well-known threat actor groups (that is, *APT29*) from searching a website such as the *MITRE* **Adversarial Tactics, Techniques, and Common Knowledge (ATT&CK)** website.

- **How do you scope out a pentesting engagement?**

The first step is typically determining why the company wants a pentest. Are they just doing the engagement to fulfill some type of legal or compliance requirement? Does the organization have an initiative to improve overall organizational security? Knowing why they want the pentest helps you understand how much buy-in you will have from their team.

- **What are some ways you can gather information on a target during a pentest?**

Some of the common ways to get information on a target include more passive activities, such as OSINT, and more active techniques, such as running a **Network Mapper (Nmap)** scan. Your specific actions will depend on the scope of the pentest. If you get this question in an interview, I would suggest asking a question back to the interviewer about the scope of the pentest because that will help guide your answer to this question.

- **What is social engineering?**

Social engineering is basically the use of human psychology to influence someone else's behavior.

Components of a successful social engineering attack include an evaluation of the target and their weaknesses, the ability to perform pretexting, the ability to exploit human psychology for the attacker's benefit, the ability to build a perceived relationship with the target, and the ability to get the target to take some sort of desired action.

Here's a simple example of social engineering. You and I are at a coffee shop, and I convince you to buy me a cup of coffee. Perhaps I mention I left my wallet at home because I'm stressed out that my kid is in hospital, and you feel sorry for me and buy the cup of coffee because you have little kids of your own. In this example, I'm just getting a cup of coffee, but what if I sent you an email with a malicious GoFundMe link embedded with a keylogger and used the same story about my kid in the hospital? You might click the link to donate, be redirected to the real GoFundMe page, and make a donation to help. Meanwhile, I've dropped malware on your system and now track every keystroke you make as you log in to your bank account to see whether the GoFundMe donation has registered on your account balance.

One thing to keep in mind is that during an interview, you might be asked to conduct a social engineering attack and then continue your (simulated) attack through the organization after gaining initial entry. The next steps after entry can include things such as enumerating user accounts on the system to identify administrator accounts, privilege escalation, network enumeration, deploying ransomware, and enumerating Active Directory with a tool such as BloodHound (`https://github.com/BloodHoundAD/BloodHound`).

- **What are some ways to perform physical pentesting?**

  Before answering this question, it's usually best to start with a short overview of what could happen if physical security were breached. If you breach the physical security of a target, you could steal devices, documents, and data, take photographs or videos of restricted areas or proprietary systems and additional security defenses being used to protect them, and then plant things such as keyloggers (via a **Universal Serial Bus (USB)** drop attack) and set up rogue devices on the target's network.

  Common physical security controls that are put in place to stop attackers include door locks (physical/electronic), surveillance cameras and security alarms, security guards, perimeter walls and gates, security lights, motion sensors, and mantraps.

  Physical pentesting can include dumpster diving, lock picking, cloning badges, bypassing motion detectors, jumping fences or walls, bypassing or interrupting the feeds of surveillance, cameras, and **radio-frequency identification (RFID)** replay attacks.

- **What are the types of social engineering?**

  There are several types of social engineering attacks, including the following:

  - **Phishing attacks** are typically done via email whereby the attacker is looking to obtain sensitive information or get the recipient to perform a specific action (such as transfer money to a bank account controlled by the attacker). There are several forms of phishing attacks, such as these:

    - **Phishing emails** are the most common form of phishing attacks, and you will typically see them done against a broad range of targets—in the case of spam— or more narrowly focused—in the case of **business email compromise** (**BEC**) attacks. BEC attacks usually involve spear-phishing and whaling. Phishing attacks are the most common entry point of attacks, including ransomware attacks.

    - **Spear-phishing attacks** are targeted phishing attacks against a specific person or group. The attacker would need to gain information about the target and craft a message, across any medium, that would entice the victim to take some sort of action. An example would be the attacker knowing you love drinking coffee from Starbucks. Through social media posts, the attacker identifies two locations you typically go to and then sends you a coupon link through social media for a free cup of coffee at one of those locations. In one of my training programs, a student was able to get an instructor to click a fake link with a similar type of attack for a free donut. Fortunately for the instructor, this was done in a controlled setting and the link was not really malicious.

    - Another example of a spear-phishing attack is the threat actor noticing employees at a company order from the same restaurant at lunch each day and then compromising the restaurant's website with malware so that each employee visiting the website gets their system infected. This is known as a **watering-hole attack**.

    - **Whaling attacks** are another form of a targeted phishing attack. The main difference between whaling attacks and spear-phishing attacks is that a whaling attack focuses on a powerful or wealthy individual, such as the **chief executive officer** (**CEO**) of a major company. A whaling attack is often harder to pull off successfully, but the financial reward for the attacker could be in the millions.

- **Tailgating** is another social engineering attack where the adversary gains access to a secure area by following an authorized employee in. In this case, the employee does not know the attacker has followed them in, and this can happen if the employee opens the door wide or if it takes time for the door to close after the authorized employee. This attack is hard to pull off if there are security guards or if the authorized employee is situationally aware.

- **Piggybacking** is an attack whereby the victim is tricked into letting the attacker in. This can happen a lot at larger companies, where the attacker mentions they work in a different department and just forgot their badge at home. Forgetting a badge or other employee ID happens a lot in companies, and many employees would empathize with the attacker and let them in the door.

I worked at a healthcare organization where every day, someone would forget their badge to scan in and wait at the door for someone else to let them in. Even back then, I implemented zero trust and would decline to let the person in, even if they worked in my department. My argument was that I didn't know whether HR had fired them last night and they were unauthorized to be in the building. Needless to say, that didn't make me popular with some coworkers, but they did understand my point of view a few months later when a man with a gun was able to gain entry into the building because someone else thought he worked there and had just forgotten his badge.

Some other attacks you might see referenced in certification study material are hoaxes, elicitation, spam, and impersonation. In my experience, these are normally coupled with the previous ones mentioned. For example, a hoax is simply where the attacker presents a fictitious situation. An example of this is when you receive a phishing email from your *bank* stating there is an issue with your account, and you need to verify your identity by logging in to your account from a link in the email. If you click the link, you are taken to a fake login page that will capture your username and password.

- **How can a company protect against social engineering attacks?**

  Some ways to help protect against social engineering attacks are **two-factor authentication (2FA)**, security awareness training, granular access control, logical controls (such as blocking USB ports on hosts), and proper security policies.

  When I did security awareness training for healthcare companies, I would always relate each recommendation to how it impacted the employees' day. For example, I would ask the nursing staff what would happen to their license if they shared their login credentials with me and I went in and altered 90% of their nursing notes on patients. How would they know which notes I had altered? What would local, state, and federal agencies do to them and their license? How would it impact their patients and the care that they received? When you put training into context for people, they are more likely to follow best practices.

- **What is the content of a well-written pentest report?**

  A pentest report is important and should contain the following items:

  - A cover page.

  - An executive summary should be one page or less and should highlight exciting pieces of the report's findings. Think of this part as marketing, and you need to get the stakeholder to buy what you are selling so that they finish reading the full report.

  - A summary of vulnerabilities that you found. A simple pie-chart graphic works well for this if you categorize the vulnerabilities.

  - Details of the testing team and tools that were used in the engagement.

  - A copy of the original scope of work that was signed as part of the contract. It's helpful to have this in the report as a reference for the client.

  - The main body content of the report that goes into detail in terms of your findings.

- **How can you identify whether a web application that you came across might be vulnerable to a blind Structured Query Language (SQL) injection attack?**

  You can use the `sleep` command, and if the web app sleeps for a period of time, it could indicate it is vulnerable.

- **What is a MITM attack?**

  In a **man-in-the-middle (MITM)** attack, the attacker acts as a relay between the client and the server. You can use things such as **HyperText Transfer Protocol (HTTP) Strict Transport Security (HSTS)** and digital signatures of packets to protect against MITM attacks. Some popular tools for performing MITM attacks are Wireshark, Ettercap, Nmap, Metasploit, and Netcat.

- **What is CSRF?**

  Cross-Site Request Forgery (CSRF) attacks take advantage of the trust relationship that is established between the user and a website. The attacker uses stored authentication in browser cookies on the user's side to authenticate to the website. An example is you have a login to a shopping website and you store the authentication in cookies in your web browser so that each time you visit the shopping website, it authenticates you and takes you into your account. An attacker could craft a **Uniform Resource Locator (URL)** with a parameter to increase the number of items added to your shopping cart when you are purchasing an item. You might not notice this and end up purchasing the additional items.

- **What is an open redirect attack?**

  In an open redirect attack, the parameter values of the HTTP `GET` request allow information to be entered that can redirect the user to a different website. The redirect could happen once on the loading of the website page or after the user has taken an action such as logging in to the site.

  In this example, the `RelayState` parameter is not being validated by the website, so an attacker could replace the legitimate website with their malicious one and the user would be redirected to the malicious site.

  Correct URL: `https://www.microsoft.com/login.html?RelayState=http%3A%2F%2FMicrosoftGear.com%2Fnext`

  Attacker URL: `https://www.microsoft.com/login.html?RelayState=http%3A%2F%2FBadGuyWebsite.com`

  This type of attack is commonly used in phishing emails, where the victim is redirected to a fake login page (for their bank, PayPal, and so on) after clicking a link in the email. After they enter their login credentials, the victim is then redirected to the real website and asked to enter their login credentials again.

- **Which cookie security flags exist?**

  The `HttpOnly` flag can be used to block access to the cookie from the client side, which can mitigate XSS attacks.

  The `Secure` flag forces cookies to be transported over **HTTP Secure (HTTPS)** instead of HTTP.

- **How do you bypass common file upload restrictions in web applications?**

  One way to bypass restrictions is using Burp Suite to intercept and alter the request parameters to bypass the restriction.

- **What is the last pentest tool that you've improved, fixed, and/or contributed to?**

  This question is targeted toward experienced pentesters, and it's designed to help the hiring manager identify how you are giving back to the community.

- **What is a Boolean blind SQL injection attack?**

  In a Boolean blind SQL injection attack, the attacker sends a SQL query to the database to identify a `true` or `false` response. If the database is vulnerable to a SQL injection attack, it will not return any information, and the attacker can then send a query with a `true` condition, such as `1=1`.

- **If you were able to successfully carry out the preceding blind SQL injection attack and gained access to the company network, where would you go from there?**

  This question is designed to test your methodology. After gaining initial access and establishing a shell, I would enumerate the **domain controllers (DCs)** and domain using something such as BloodHound. Next, I would dump local password hashes and do a password spray attack (using something such as Mimikatz) to gain access to a machine with a domain admin token. I would then establish a session with a DC and dump credentials to gain domain account admin access and then continue causing chaos from there. A domain admin account allows me to control virtually anything that is integrated with or controlled by Active Directory.

- **Can you identify the most common HTTP methods and how they can be used in attacks against web applications?**

  Common HTTP methods include GET, POST, PUT, DELETE, and TRACE. GET and POST are used in attacks by modifying the parameters. An attacker could use PUT to upload arbitrary files on the web server. DELETE could be used in a **denial-of-service (DoS)** attack. TRACE could be used to return the entire HTTP request, which would include cookies. An attacker could leverage TRACE to perform a **cross-site tracing (XST)** attack where the attacker uses XSS to retrieve HttpOnly cookies and authorization headers.

- **What are the differences between attacking a web application and an application programming interface (API)?**

  Web applications have traditionally been one request to one server, so you just needed to protect one application. With APIs, you have hundreds of requests to hundreds of microservices, which means you now have to protect hundreds of small applications. The main API security flaws being exploited are around authentication and authorization, and each microservice needs to verify identity and permissions before granting access. A challenge in API security is visibility into your APIs because shadow APIs might exist (those that developers have forgotten about), and if they are public-facing, they can be exploited.

- **Describe the last business logic vulnerability that you found.**

  Business logic vulnerabilities are weaknesses in the design and/or implementation of an application. An example of a business logic vulnerability is an application that cannot handle unexpected input from a user properly, such as a banking application that allowed a negative value when transferring money between accounts. An attacker might then leverage this vulnerability to remove money from the victim's account.

- **How do you measure the results of a pentest?**

  It depends on what the organization is looking to measure. Common things to track are the criticality of findings, how many issues that surfaced in the pentest actually get fixed, what types of vulnerabilities and exploits are being discovered, and which new issues have been identified since the last pentest.

- **What are the phases of pentesting?**

  This question could have different answers, depending on the hiring manager having real pentesting experience or just passing a few knowledge-based certification exams.

If you go by the **penetration testing execution standard** (PTES), there are seven phases of pentesting, which are *pre-engagement, intelligence gathering, threat modeling, vulnerability analysis, exploitation, post-exploitation*, and *reporting*.

If you take a popular knowledge-based certification exam, the phases are *reconnaissance, scanning and enumeration, gaining access, maintaining access*, and *covering tracks*.

- **How can you leverage threat modeling in a pentest?**

Threat modeling helps the pentester identify critical business assets and the impact on the organization if those assets are compromised by an attacker. It also helps you identify threat actors most likely to target the organization. This helps the pentester better prioritize vulnerabilities found during the engagement.

- **Compare bug bounty programs and a pentest.**

Bug bounty programs can typically find more vulnerabilities over time than a pentest because they involve continuous testing. You will also get a more diverse group of skill sets, and the payouts of many bug bounty programs are far less than the cost of a single pentest.

- **What is an HTTP Desync attack?**

HTTP Desync attacks abuse the method in which a chain of HTTP servers interpret consecutive requests, especially around the boundaries of requests. As an example, an attacker could send a request with a transfer-encoding header that doesn't meet values specified in **Request for Comments** (RFC) *7230*. This can help the attacker hide the encoding of their payload from the WAF.

- **What is the difference between vertical and horizontal privilege escalation?**

Horizontal privilege escalation refers to bypassing the authentication mechanism for users that have the same level of privilege and taking over their accounts. Vertical privilege escalation refers to escalating privilege to a higher level of access, such as a standard user now having the same level of access as the administrator account.

- **How often should organizations have an external pentest performed?**

This answer depends on their compliance requirements, but generally, this should happen at least once a year and preferably on a quarterly basis. One thing you will notice when you're working as a pentester is that many companies will not fix any of the issues you report, so you might come back a year later and identify the same issues.

- **What are the legal considerations for pentests?**

  For pentests, you need to have a contract in place before starting the engagement. The contract is often referred to as your *get-out-of-jail-free card*, but keep in mind that you could still be arrested for performing a pentest even if it's authorized.

  Some other key legal considerations are outlined here:

  - Does the client really own the systems and/or applications they want you to test?

  - Will the client assume liability for any interruptions or damage that occur as a result of the pentest, or are you responsible?

  - What happens when third-party data or services are damaged as a result of the pentest? Who is responsible?

  - Do you need a private investigator license to perform a pentest?

  - Which jurisdiction will be recognized for the pentest? For example, if you are testing offices in Alabama and Virginia, which state's laws will apply to the engagement?

  - Who owns any new methods or tools that are developed as a result of the pentest engagement?

  - Is there a duty to warn third parties about pentest results based on the findings? For example, you discover a high-severity zero-day exploit as a result of a pentest. Do you report it?

- **Which common vulnerabilities can you exploit in pentests?**

  This can include things such as default or weak credentials, credential reuse (credential stuffing attacks), security misconfigurations (this happens a lot with cloud environments), poor patch management practices, and social engineering of the organization's staff. When I worked as a pentester, I found that I had greater success in engagements by targeting the human element (*layer 8*) than focusing on the technical side.

- **What is a buffer overflow attack?**

  Buffers are memory storage regions that temporarily hold data while it is being transferred from one location to another. A buffer overflow occurs when the volume of data exceeds the storage capacity of the memory buffer. As a result, the program attempting to write the data to the buffer overwrites adjacent memory locations.

  For example, a buffer for login credentials may be designed to expect username and password inputs of 8 bytes, so if a transaction involves an input of 10 bytes (that is, 2 bytes more than expected), the program may write the excess data past the buffer boundary.

As you can see, the questions you might be asked during an interview for pentester roles can vary, but the main thing to keep in mind is that for more junior-level roles, the interview is typically focused on knowledge with a small hands-on component. For more senior-level interviews, you can expect a more hands-on interview.

Summary

In this chapter, you learned what a pentester is, the average salaries in the US for pentesting, and common questions you might be asked during an interview. It's important to remember that the questions listed in this chapter cover entry-level through principal pentester roles, so you might not be asked all questions from this chapter during your job interview.

In the next chapter, we will learn about malware analyst careers.

4
Digital Forensic Analyst

In this chapter, you will learn what a digital forensic analyst is and the average salary range for this career in the **United States** (**US**). You will also learn about career progression options and learn common interview questions for the role.

The following topics will be covered in this chapter:

- What is a digital forensic analyst?
- How much can you make in this career?
- Which other career paths can you choose after working as a digital forensic analyst?
- Common interview questions for a digital forensic analyst career

What is a digital forensic analyst?

Digital forensic analysts are tasked with collecting, preserving, and analyzing digital evidence. They might work with **incident response teams** (**IRTs**) to investigate incidents and attempt to identify threat actors responsible for an attack. Digital forensic analysts may also work with law enforcement agencies to help in criminal investigations, including crimes against children, and help companies in civil and administrative investigations. They may also be hired by law firms to conduct **electronic discovery** (**e-discovery**) work, where the analyst collects electronic evidence to be used in civil cases. An example of this might be collecting evidence on the financial activity of one spouse during a divorce proceeding to help the attorneys prove how much money they have in their accounts. As a digital forensic analyst, you will analyze operating systems such as Windows, macOS, Linux, and mobile OSs, analyze volatile and non-volatile data, and work with forensic tools such as EnCase and Autopsy (`https://www.sleuthkit.org/autopsy/`).

The **Digital Forensics and Incident Response** (**DFIR**) *Diva* blog (`https://dfirdiva.com/`) contains listings of free and low-cost resources for you to gain hands-on experience in conducting forensic investigations.

How much can you make in this career?

The salary range for a digital forensic analyst in the US depends on a number of factors, such as your location, the size of the company you work for, certifications you hold, college degrees, and your skills. In the US, an average salary to expect is between $72,000 and $94,000. If you work in an IRT and have some experience, your base salary in the US may be in the six-figure range.

Which other career paths can you choose after working as a digital forensic analyst?

The skills learned as a digital forensic analyst can prepare you for other careers such as penetration tester, malware analyst, cybersecurity manager, and senior executive roles as you advance in your career, such as **chief information security officer** (**CISO**). As a digital forensic analyst, you can also use your skills to work on an IRT.

Common interview questions for a digital forensic analyst career

In this section, you will learn some of the most common interview questions that are posed in relation to digital forensic analyst jobs. We present a list of these here:

- **Why did you decide to pursue a career in digital forensics?**

  I suggest you answer this one honestly. What really interests you about working in forensics? Is it the opportunity to catch people doing bad things? Is it because you watched some episodes of *CSI: Crime Scene Investigation* and found digital forensics interesting?

  My answer to this question would be that I fought against bad people all over the world in the military and wanted to continue tracking down bad people while helping the innocent people of the world.

- **What is the chain of custody (CoC)?**

  The CoC is documentation that tracks evidence from the initial scene through the evidence being presented in a court of law. The **chain of custody** should show who controls evidence and when, document each person or system that holds the evidence at each stage of the investigative process, and document the evidence analysis and any disposal of evidence during or after the investigation. You can view an example of a chain of custody form at this link: `https://www.nist.gov/document/sample-chain-custody-formdocx`.

- **Which tools can be used to recover deleted files?**

  Some tools that could be used to recover your deleted files include EaseUS (`https://www.easeus.com/`), Advanced Recovery, Disk Drill (`https://www.cleverfiles.com/data-recovery-software.html`), Recoverit (`https://recoverit.wondershare.com/`), and Recuva (`https://www.ccleaner.com/recuva`).

- **What is hashing?**

  Hashing is a one-way function that takes a specific input and maps it to a specific output. As an example, let's say I use the 26 letters of the US English language alphabet for the input and I map each of those letters sequentially to each corresponding number, so if I enter an *A*, then my output would be a 1, and if I enter a *B*, then my output would be a 2. Hashing is something you use to verify the integrity of the file or information. If you download files from websites such as `kali.org`, you will see a hash for the original file. This helps you compare and validate the original file from the vendor and the file you downloaded to ensure a malicious actor did not alter the file.

- **Can you provide examples of some common hashing algorithms?**

  Some common hashing algorithms in use right now are **Message Digest 5 (MD5)**, **Secure Hash Algorithm 256 (SHA-256)**, and SHA-512.

- **What is data carving?**

  Data carving is conducted in a forensic investigation to identify deleted information on a system. Some forensic tools offer data-carving capabilities, and these typically identify file headers and footers to recover files that are intact, meaning the files have been deleted but not overwritten yet by new data. As a forensic investigator, you may also conduct manual data carving, whereby you can pull fragments from previous files in slack space.

- **What is data mining?**

  Data mining is just the process of pulling out specific information from large datasets. In digital forensics, mining can be used to collect correlating data on a suspect. As an example, a suspect visits an internet café to use its computers to commit criminal activity. Let's pretend the internet café doesn't have user accounts, so the only way to identify the person responsible for the crimes is to collect information from the computer, including timestamps, and then correlate that information with security cameras in the area to narrow down the suspect list and identify the person committing the illegal activity.

- **What is steganography?**

  Steganography is a way to hide information within another source. For example, a criminal might hide **child sexual abuse material (CSAM)** images within an image of a dog found on the web. The average person would see the image in the search results and just think it was a picture of a dog, but other criminals would know to use a steganalysis tool to pull the CSAM images out.

- **What are some considerations around forensic investigations in the cloud?**

  Considerations include jurisdiction, **cloud service providers (CSPs)**, and multi-tenancy. CSPs host data all over the world, which causes jurisdictional issues. For example, you might work with law enforcement in the US and have a warrant to seize data on a suspect, but the data might be stored in Russia, which doesn't recognize your warrant. Another consideration is the CSPs themselves, as they control the hardware and the logging capability in **platform-as-a-service (PaaS)** and **software-as-a-service (SaaS)** deployments. CSPs might also sanitize log files from customers and have policies restricting access to log files. Multi-tenancy is another challenge because other organizations do not want you as an investigator to accidentally access their data from the cloud.

- **Can you name some common encryption algorithms that are used to encrypt data?**

  Some encryption algorithms are **Advanced Encryption Standard (AES)**, **Rivest-Shamir-Adleman (RSA)**, and **Triple Data Encryption Standard (3DES)**. 3DES is still used by some financial institutions. RSA is resource-intensive and is usually only used to encrypt small amounts of data. AES is what you will see more commonly used over the others.

- **Can you retrieve data from an encrypted hard drive?**

  Yes, but to view the data you will need the decryption key.

- **What is SIFT?**

  The **Sans Investigative Forensic Toolkit (SIFT)** is a forensic workstation from SANS that comes with a number of pre-installed forensic and IR tools. Using pre-made images such as SIFT and the Volatility (`https://github.com/volatilityfoundation/volatility`) framework can save you time in setting up your forensic investigation lab.

- **What is timeline analysis?**

  Timeline analysis is a sequence of events on a system or group of systems that allow the investigator to see what happened and when, along with which events happened just before or after an incident.

- **What is metadata?**

  Metadata is commonly known as data about data. There are three types of metadata, which are **descriptive**, **administrative**, and **structural**. Descriptive metadata contains information about a file, such as the file author, keywords, and title. Administrative metadata contains the ownership and rights management of a file and which program was used to create the file. Structural metadata contains relational information on file data. In digital forensics, metadata can be used to identify the security settings of a file, and in the case of an email thread, metadata can be used to track the email origin and which other systems the email has passed through to its destination.

- **Analyze the following scenario and determine the best course of action.**

  You are contacted by the IRT in your company that a host system has been beaconing out to a **command and control (C2)** server. The IRT has blocked the outbound communication and requested for you to collect and analyze the disk. Upon arrival at the workstation, what is the first thing you should do?

  The first step you should take is to document the current scene, including taking photographs of the workstation and surrounding area and documenting everything that is evidence before touching anything.

- **How do you get indicators of compromise (IOCs) from analyzing malware samples?**

  You can get IOCs by using static analysis. The first step should be to obtain a hash of the malware file and then search online databases, such as VirusTotal, to see whether anyone else has already done a write-up on the malware sample. This step can save you hours of frustration in your investigation. You can then use a tool such as Sysinternals (`https://docs.microsoft.com/en-us/sysinternals/`) coupled with `regex` to analyze the strings of the malware sample to look for **Internet Protocol (IP)** addresses, suspicious **Uniform Resource Locators (URLs)**, and file paths. If you are not familiar with using the Sysinternals suite, this YouTube video (`https://www.youtube.com/watch?v=vW8eAqZyWeo`) from Mark Russinovich provides an overview of using Sysinternals for malware analysis.

- **What is the difference between static and dynamic malware analysis?**

  Static malware analysis is used to analyze the malware sample and its code without executing it. The forensic investigator might be limited in seeing what capabilities the malware has with simple static analysis, so dynamic malware analysis is used to analyze the behavior of the malware sample. More advanced static analysis can be used to dissect the malware down to assembly language, but this reverse engineering is time-consuming and not pragmatic for many investigations that are part of IR.

- **What is a PE file?**

  Portable executable (PE) is the standard Windows file format for executable files, **dynamic-link libraries (DLLs)**, and object code for both 32-bit and 64-bit Windows operating systems.

- **How would a piece of malware maintain persistence?**

  A few ways to maintain persistence are listed here: the malware copies itself to the Windows `Startup` folder so that it executes every time you reboot the system; adding entries to the RunOnce and Run Windows registry keys; abusing the default of file associations.

- **Can you name some items you would carry in your forensic response kit?**

  The contents of a forensic response kit will vary based on the investigator, but some items you will want to include are antistatic bags, your forensic laptop, dongles, screwdriver toolkit, extra cables, Faraday bags or commercial aluminum foil, write blocking devices, storage media, gloves, a digital camera for recording the condition of the scene when you arrive, notepad, and evidence paperwork such as labels or tags and CoC forms.

- **What are the two main types of data you deal with as a digital forensic investigator?**

  The two main types of data are volatile and non-volatile.

- **What is volatile data?**

  Volatile data is temporary data on your digital device that is dependent upon having a steady power supply. If the power is interrupted at all, this data can be lost. Some examples of volatile data include the system time, a listing of users logged on to the system, a list of files that are open, information on the network, information on processes running on the system, process-to-port mapping, services running, a list of drivers on the system, a history of the command run on the system, and the contents of the clipboard.

- **What is non-volatile data?**

  Non-volatile data is data that will remain on the system, even if the power supply is interrupted. This type of data can be stored on secondary storage devices, such as memory cards and a hard disk. Examples of non-volatile data include slack space, hidden files, swap files, the `index.dat` file, clusters that are unallocated, partitions that are not being used, your registry settings, and system event logs.

- **Can you name some other locations you can look in to identify information that is similar to the data that would have been in random-access memory (RAM) if the RAM evidence is not collected prior to the suspect's device being turned off?**

  Some additional locations include the hibernation file (`hiberfill.sys`), the pagefile (`pagefile.sys`), the swapfile (`swapfile.sys`), and the memory dump (`memory.dmp`).

- **Can you provide examples of artifacts you can get from analyzing RAM?**

  Some artifact information you can get from analyzing RAM includes encryption keys, passwords, IP addresses, browsing history, cleartext data, configuration information, and commands that were entered.

- **In which situations can duplicate evidence suffice as evidence?**

  Situations in which duplicate evidence will be accepted include if the original evidence is destroyed due to a fire, flood, or other disaster in the normal course of business. Duplicate evidence can also be used if the original evidence is in the possession of a third party.

- **Can you name three categories of cases you might investigate?**

  Three types of cases are civil, criminal, and administrative. A case you are investigating might fall into all three categories.

- **Which amendment in the US protects against illegal search and seizure by government authorities?**

  The Fourth Amendment.

- **What is the primary purpose of the first responder?**

  The main goal of the first responder is to secure the scene until investigators arrive. This is done to help protect evidence from contamination or theft.

- **Can you provide examples of some forensic tools?**

  A few forensic tools are FTK Imager, Autopsy, EnCase, **Forensic Recovery of Evidence Device** (**FRED**), Capsa, FileMerlin, password-cracking tools, Recuva, PALADIN, Recover My Files, Advanced Disk Recovery, and UndeletePlus.

- **What is FTK Imager?**

  FTK Imager is a popular forensic tool that helps an investigator acquire and analyze the files and folders found on system hard drives, network drives, and **compact disc read-only memory** (**CD-ROM**)/**digital versatile disc** (**DVD**). The tool also helps investigators analyze forensic images and memory dumps. Some other capabilities of FTK Imager include the ability to create hashes of files, recover and review deleted files from the Recycle Bin in the Microsoft Windows operating system, and export files and folders from captured forensic images to disk.

- **What is EnCase?**

  EnCase is a multi-purpose digital forensic platform that includes many useful tools to support your digital forensic investigation.

- **Which law in the US deals with fraud and related activity in connection with computers?**

  Title 18 US Code subsection 1030—or, more appropriately written, *18 USC §1030*—deals with fraud and other activity in connection with computers.

- **Which federal law in the US covers CSAM?**

  Title 18 US Code subsection 2252A (*18 USC §2252A*) covers CSAM.

- **What is Rule 402 of the Federal Rules of Evidence?**

  Rule 402 covers the general admissibility of relevant evidence.

- **What is the difference between Rules 701 and 702?**

  Rule 702 covers testimony by expert witnesses and *Rule 701* covers opinion testimony by laypersons.

- **Which rule would cover the admissibility of duplicates for evidence?**

  Rule 1003 covers the admissibility of duplicates. Duplicate evidence (or a copy of evidence) might be used in a situation where law enforcement cannot obtain the original evidence or if the original evidence was destroyed as part of the normal investigative process.

- **What are some best practices for computer forensic investigations?**

  The following list details a few best practices:

  - Obtain authorization to conduct the forensic investigation.
  - Conduct a preliminary analysis of the scene and identify the evidence you will be collecting.
  - Do not turn the computer off or on, run any programs, or attempt to access data on the computer before documenting the scene.
  - Collect and secure any relevant media, including hard drives, cell phones, DVDs, **Universal Serial Bus (USB)** drives, and so on that may be relevant to the investigation.
  - Conduct a bit-for-bit copy of the evidence (if possible).
  - Document in your CoC.

- **What are the steps in computer forensics investigation methodology?**

  Here is the approach we can use for investigating digital evidence:

  A.   Initial response to the scene (first response)

  B.   Search and seizure

  C.   Collect the evidence

  D.   Secure the evidence

  E.   Data acquisition

  F.   Data analysis

  G.   Evidence assessment

  H.   Documentation and reporting

  I.   Expert witness testimony

- **If an investigator needs to obtain information from a service provider (SP), such as billing records and subscriber information of a victim's computer, what type of warrant is issued?**

  An **SP search warrant** allows the investigator or first responder to obtain victim information such as billing records and subscriber information.

- **What is a platter?**

  Platters are circular metal disks that are mounted in the drive enclosure.

- **What are sectors?**

Sectors are small, physical storage units located on the hard disk platter; they are 512 bytes long.

- **What is slack space?**

When a filesystem allocates an entire cluster for a file, but the file size is much smaller than the full cluster available, the remaining area is known as slack space.

- **What is a GUID?**

A **globally unique identifier** (**GUID**) is a 128-bit unique number generated by Windows that is used to identify things such as **Component Object Model** (**COM**) DLLs, primary key values, browser sessions, and usernames. A GUID is sometimes known as a **universally unique ID** (**UUID**).

- **What is file carving?**

File carving is a technique used to recover files and fragments of files from an unallocated portion of the hard disk. This technique can be used if you can't find any file metadata.

- **What type of image file format is lossless?**

Portable Network Graphics (**PNG**) is a lossless image format that was intended to replace **Graphics Interchange Format** (**GIF**) and **Tagged Image File Format** (**TIFF**) formats.

- **What type of image file starts with a hexadecimal (hex) value of FF D8 FF?**

Joint Photographic Experts Group (**JPEG**) files start with this hex format.

- **What is the Master Boot Record (MBR)?**

The MBR holds information about partitions, the bootloader code, and information on filesystems.

- **Can you explain the boot process?**

The boot process starts with the **Power-On Self-Test** (**POST**), where the **central processing unit** (**CPU**) accesses the ROM and **Basic Input/Output System** (**BIOS**) or **Unified Extensible Firmware Interface** (**UEFI**) on newer computers. If the computer uses BIOS, then the BIOS will check for the MBR, and once it is located, it will activate the bootloader, then pass control to the operating system to finish booting the computer. If the computer uses UEFI, it will look for the **GUID Partition Table** (**GPT**) and then activate the bootloader, before passing control to the operating system to complete the boot process.

- **What is a registry hive?**

  A registry hive is a grouping of subkeys, values, and keys found in the Windows Registry.

- **Can you explain the difference between the modified timestamp and the change timestamp?**

  A modified timestamp shows when the content of the file has been modified, while a change timestamp shows when characteristics of the file have changed, such as permissions, the name of the file, or file ownership.

- **What is the difference between UEFI and BIOS?**

  One difference is that UEFI offers Secure Boot, which protects against your computer booting unsigned or unauthorized applications. UEFI also offers faster boot time, supports larger drives, and can run in 32-bit or 64-bit mode. BIOS runs in 16-bit mode.

- **Which National Institute of Standards and Technology (NIST) document covers sanitation techniques for the media?**

  NIST **Special Publication (SP)** *800-88* guidelines cover proper techniques for sanitizing media.

- **What is live data acquisition?**

  This is the process of acquiring volatile data (for example, RAM) from a computer that is turned on, but that is either locked or in sleep mode. You conduct live data acquisition (sometimes called live box forensics) to acquire volatile data because volatile data is lost when the system suffers a power outage or when the user turns the system off.

- **Why would you use write protection when acquiring evidence?**

  Write protection is used when acquiring images, so you do not alter the original data.

- **Can you name some functions that are offered with dcfldd and not dd?**

  Some of the functions offered are status output, hashing on the fly, flexible disk wipes, verifying a target drive is a bit-for-bit match, outputting to multiple disks or files at the same time, splitting output into multiple files with additional configurability, and piping the output.

- **Can you name some anti-forensic techniques?**

  Some common anti-forensic techniques include using encryption, data cleaning, using packers such as **Ultimate Packer for eXecutables (UPX)**, using **The Onion Router (TOR)**, altering timestamps, and using steganography.

  UPX is used to compress files. A threat actor might use a packer such as this to try to get their malware past security tools that are scanning for specific file signatures.

  The TOR browser is used to anonymize the internet activity of a user. This can be helpful for journalists in oppressive regimes. A threat actor might use TOR during their attack to obfuscate their actual IP address.

  Steganography is simply a way to hide a message within something else. For example, a threat actor might hide illegal images within a normal image file or hide a written message within an image file.

- **Where is email stored in Thunderbird?**

  Email is stored within an MBOX file. An MBOX file is just a collection of email messages from the Mozilla Thunderbird email application that are stored in a single file.

- **Where is the Google Chrome history file located?**

  The history file in Chrome is found in `%USERS%/AppData/Local/Google/Chrome/User Data/`.

- **What information can you gather from the Chrome history file?**

  Some information that can be obtained from the history file includes any typed URLs, keyword searching, and downloads of files.

- **What does the HKEY_CLASSES_ROOT registry key contain?**

  It contains the file extension association information and **programmatic ID** (`ProgID`), `class ID` (`CLSID`), and **interface ID** (`IID`) data.

- **What does the HKEY_CURRENT_USER registry contain?**

  This registry key contains the configuration information (that is, wallpaper preference, screen colors, display settings) related to the user currently logged on.

- **What does the HKEY_USERS registry key contain?**

  This registry key contains information about all the active user profiles on the system.

- **Which tools can be used to analyze Windows Registry?**

  Some tools you could use are regedit, RegRipper, **Process Monitor** (**ProcMon**), Registry Viewer, and ProDiscover.

- **Can you provide a registry key that threat actors frequently add malicious entries to in order to maintain persistence?**

  The *Run* key often has malicious entries. For example, APT29 commonly adds a spool.exe entry to the registry key.

- **What sort of data should you collect in the event of a website attack?**

  Some data that should be collected includes the following:

  - The date and time at which **HyperText Transfer Protocol** (**HTTP**) requests were sent
  - The source IP address of the request
  - Which HTTP method was used (GET, POST, and so on)
  - HTTP query information
  - A full set of HTTP headers and the full HTTP request body
  - Any event logs
  - Any file listings and timestamps

- **Can you briefly explain the MySQL architecture?**

  MySQL is a **relational database management system** (**RDBMS**) that allows you to manage large databases using **Structured Query Language** (**SQL**) queries. The MySQL architecture consists of a client layer, a storage layer, and a server layer.

- **What is database forensics?**

  Database forensics is the examination of databases and related metadata using forensically sound practices to ensure the findings are admissible in a court of law.

- **Where does the Microsoft SQL (MSSQL) server store data and logs?**

  It stores them in primary data files (**Main Database Files**, or **MDFs**), secondary data files (**SQL Server Secondary Database Files**, or **NDFs**), and transaction log data files (**Log Database Files**, or **LDFs**).

- **In which directory does the MySQL Server store status and log files?**

  It stores status and log files, along with other data managed by the server, under the data directory.

- **What are some common types of cloud models?**

  Common types include public, private, community, and hybrid.

- **Can you list the categories of cloud crimes?**

  The categories of cloud crimes are listed here:

  - **Cloud as a subject**, which refers to a crime in which attackers try to compromise the security of a cloud environment to steal data or inject malware—for example, stealing credentials of a cloud account and leveraging the credentials to delete or modify data stored in the cloud environment.

  - **Cloud as an object,** which refers to an attacker leveraging the cloud environment to conduct an attack against the CSPs. **Distributed Denial of Service (DDoS)** attacks are an example of an attack that is leveraged against CSPs.

  - **Cloud as a tool**, which refers to when an attacker uses one compromised cloud account to attack other accounts. In these situations, the source and destinations of the attack can yield evidence for your case.

- **What are some common cloud threats?**

  Some common threats involved in using cloud environments include data breaches, data loss, abuse of native cloud services for attacks, insecure **application programming interfaces (APIs)**, security misconfigurations, a lack of accountability for keeping data safe, not clearly identifying who owns the responsibility for the security of data, a lack of user ID federation, lack of visibility, multi-tenancy security concerns, and a lack of compliance.

- **Can you provide examples of crimes that are supported by email capabilities?**

  Some crimes include **business email compromise (BEC)**, identity theft, cyberstalking, and crimes targeting children.

- **Can you name some tools used for collecting and analyzing emails?**

  Tools that can be used for email collection and analysis include Stellar Phoenix Deleted Email Recovery, FTK, Paraben E-mail Examiner, and Kernel for Outlook PST Recovery.

- **What is the purpose of the Stellar Phoenix Deleted Email Recovery software?**

  It helps you recover lost or deleted emails from MS Outlook data (**Personal Storage Table**, or **PST**) files and **Outlook Express Mail Database (DBX)** files.

  Paraben's E-mail Examiner helps you examine different email formats, including Outlook (PST and **Offline Storage Table (OST)**), Thunderbird, Outlook Express, Windows Mail, and more. The tool allows the analysis of message headers, bodies, and attachments. It also helps recover email from deleted folders, offers support for advanced searching and reporting, and offers an export capability to PST and other formats.

- **What information can you find on a subscriber identity module (SIM) card?**

  You can locate information such as contacts, messages, timestamps, **integrated circuit card ID (ICCID)**, the last numbers dialed, and the SP name.

- **What is the International Mobile Equipment Identifier (IMEI)?**

  The IMEI is a 15-digit unique number on the handset that identifies mobile equipment.

- **In which locations can you find evidence on mobile devices?**

  Some locations include the internal memory, the external memory, and the SIM card.

- **Can you name a tool that can be used to gather information from Facebook and Twitter?**

  Bulk Extractor is one tool that can be used to collect and analyze social media artifacts from a captured memory file or forensic image.

- **What are some benefits of solid-state drives (SSDs)?**

  In comparison to traditional hard drives, SSDs offer increased reliability, weigh less, increase the data access speed, and help reduce power consumption.

- **What is the master file table (MFT)?**

  The MFT tracks the files in the volume and essentially manages them.

There are many locations where a digital forensic investigator could find evidence on a system. For job interviews, it is important to be familiar with some of the common types of data that can be acquired and their location.

Summary

In this chapter, you learned about the job of a digital forensic analyst and what to expect in terms of an average salary. You also learned the two main types of data that can be collected in a digital forensic investigation—volatile and non-volatile data—and some of the most common interview questions you may face from a hiring manager. You also learned about some tasks and investigations you might be involved in as a digital forensic investigator.

In the next chapter, we will discuss a cryptanalyst's career path.

5
Cryptographer/ Cryptanalyst

This chapter will cover two job roles: cryptographer and cryptanalyst, which are blended under the title of cryptographer since the majority of open private sector job postings list *cryptographer* as the job title in demand. As a cryptographer, you will also be doing cryptanalyst work in attempting to break encryption. In this chapter, you will learn about what cryptographers do, where they might work, and the average salary range for cryptographers in the US. You will also learn about the career progression options and learn common interview questions for the role.

The following topics will be covered in this chapter:

- What is a cryptographer?
- How much can you make in this career?
- What other careers can you do?
- Common interview questions for cryptographers

What is a cryptographer?

Cryptographers write and crack the encryption code used to protect data. In a cryptographer role, you will help to develop better algorithms to help protect data from threats. Depending on the organization you work with, your day-to-day work will vary, but you will be protecting critical data from being stolen, deleted, altered, or copied. Cryptographers also help to develop mathematical and statistical models that can help organizations locate and disrupt threats to their systems.

Some of your day-to-day work as a cryptographer will include identifying weaknesses in existing cryptography systems and identifying ways to better secure them, conducting testing of cryptology theories, improving data security across the organization, deploying symmetric and asymmetric cryptography, managing the organization's encryption implementation especially as it relates to code and third-party products, conducting training of other departments to help them implement better encryption practices, and developing new encryption solutions.

To be successful in a cryptography career, you should have hands-on experience of operating systems and computer networking, and know at least one programming language. You will also need to be familiar with different encryption algorithms, **message authentication code** (**MAC**), hashing, number theory, key exchange, data structures, and digital signatures, and have strong mathematical skills in areas such as linear algebra. In addition to these hard skills, you will need soft skills such as the ability to work well in teams, effective communication with different stakeholders, problem-solving and critical thinking skills, and good time management skills.

Full-time cryptography roles are typically found in public sector (government) work. In the US, cryptographers might work for government entities such as the National Security Agency or the Department of Defense.

Certifications available for this career path include the **Certified Blockchain Security Professional** (**CBSP**) and the **EC-Council Certified Encryption Specialist** (**ECES**).

If you are looking to gain hands-on experience working through cryptography challenges, the Cryptopals website has free challenges around cryptography (`https://cryptopals.com/`).

SimpliLearn also has free cryptography training available on their YouTube channel at this link: `https://youtu.be/C7vmouDOJYM`.

How much can you make in this career?

According to ZipRecruiter (`https://www.ziprecruiter.com/Salaries/Cryptography-Salary`), the average salary for cryptographers in the United States is around $145,000 and varies with the organization that you work for, your location, and years of experience. With just a few years of experience, your salary in the United States can rise above $190,000.

What other careers can you do?

A career as a cryptographer can help you advance into other cybersecurity careers such as a penetration tester, an incident responder, and a malware reverse engineer. This career is also a natural progression into a crypto and blockchain security researcher career, where you may be researching emerging technology and/or threats, contributing to research publications, and developing new approaches to managing threats.

Common interview questions for cryptographers

The following questions are designed to assess your fundamental knowledge of cryptography. In job interviews, you may also be asked to solve cryptography challenges. The hands-on assessment will depend upon the employer and the role you are applying for:

- **What is the difference between cryptography, cryptology, and cryptanalysis?**

  Cryptography is the practice of secure communication techniques. **Cryptology** is the study of secure communication techniques. **Cryptanalysis** is the practice of breaking cryptography.

- **What is the difference between encoding, hashing, and encryption?**

  Encoding is just the process of converting data from one format to another. ASCII, Base64, and Unicode are examples of encoding algorithms. In encoding, the same algorithm is used to encode and decode the data, which means an attacker would just need to have the data sample to be able to decode it.

Encryption is the process of using a cryptographic key to scramble your data so it is unreadable. Symmetric encryption involves using a shared key where both the sender and receiver know the key. The shared key is then used to encrypt and decrypt the data. Asymmetric encryption uses a public and private key. The public key is known (hence the name *public*) and is used to encrypt the data, and the receiver's private key is used to decrypt the data. **Rivest-Shamir-Adleman (RSA)** is a well-known asymmetric encryption algorithm.

Hashing is a one-way function, where a string of information is run through a hashing algorithm, and it produces a fixed-length output based on the algorithm you are using and the input data. This means that if the input data and the hashing algorithm used remain the same, the output will be the same. Hashing allows you to confirm that the data has not been altered. As an example, if you download files from the Kali Linux website (`https://www.kali.org/`), you will be able to check whether the hash of the file you have downloaded is the same hash as the original file. This helps you identify whether a malicious hacker might have altered the file from their website.

- **What is the difference between asymmetric and symmetric encryption?**

Symmetric encryption uses a single private key that both the sender and receiver of the message know. An advantage of symmetric encryption is that it is faster and requires less computation power than asymmetric encryption.

In the following example, Alice wants to send an encrypted message to her friend, Bob. Alice encrypts the message with the shared, private key, which converts (encrypts) the message from the plaintext to ciphertext. When Bob receives the message, he uses the same shared, private key to decrypt the message and read the plaintext message.

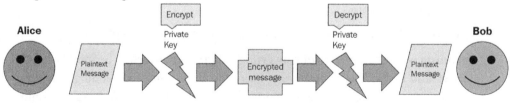

Figure 5.1 – Symmetric encryption example

Asymmetric encryption uses a public and private key. The public key is shared by the owner, but their private key must only be known by them. Asymmetric encryption provides confidentiality through encryption and provides authenticity and nonrepudiation through the use of digital signatures.

In the following example, Alice encrypts her plaintext message with Bob's shared public key and when Bob receives the message, he decrypts it with his private key (known only to him) to view the content of the message.

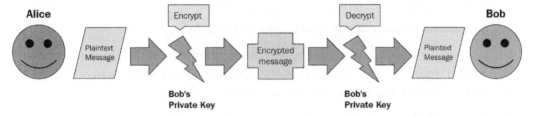

Figure 5.2 – Asymmetric encryption example

- **What are some examples of symmetric encryption algorithms?**

  Some examples are **Data Encryption Standard (DES)**, which used a 56-bit key, **Triple-DES (3DES)**, which replaced DES and used 168 bits, **International Data Encryption Algorithm (IDEA)**, Twofish, Blowfish, **Rivest Cipher (RC)**, and **Advanced Encryption Standard (AES)**, which has key sizes of 128 bits, 192 bits, and 256 bits.

- **What are some examples of asymmetric encryption algorithms?**

  Some examples are Diffie-Hellman, RSA, El Gamal, and **elliptic curve cryptography (ECC)**.

- **Name some hashing algorithms.**

  Some common hashing algorithms you should have knowledge of are the following:

  - **Message-digest algorithm version 5 (MD5)**

  - **Secure hash algorithm 1 (SHA-1)**, which has a 160-bit hash value and is no longer a standard for use across organizations

  - **Secure hash algorithm 2 (SHA-2)**, which includes the hash functions SHA-224, SHA-256, SHA-384, SHA-512, SHA-512/224, and SHA-512/256

  - **Secure hash algorithm 3 (SHA-3)**, which includes the hash functions SHA3-224, SHA3-256, SHA3-384, SHA3-512, SHAKE128, and SHAKE256

- **What is steganography?**

  Steganography is the practice of hiding messages or data within another medium. For example, you could hide a secret message in a photo of your dog using steganography.

Some tools you can use for steganography are Open Stego (`https://www.openstego.com/`), Quick Stego (`http://quickcrypto.com/free-steganography-software.html`), and the SNOW steganography tool (`https://github.com/mattkwan-zz/snow`).

- **Can you name some common cryptography attacks?**

Common cryptography attacks include known-plaintext attacks, chosen-plaintext attacks, ciphertext-only attacks, replay attacks (typically in the form of man-in-the-middle attacks), and chosen-ciphertext attacks.

- **What is PKI?**

Public key infrastructure (**PKI**) is used to describe the policies, software, and other infrastructure needed to manage digital certificates and public key encryption.

PKI is best explained with a simple example. In the following figure, our user, **Bob**, requests a certificate from a **registration authority** (**RA**). The RA then helps to validate the identity of the user and sends a request to the **certificate authority** (**CA**) to create a user certificate and keys. Once the CA has created the certificate and keys, it sends it to the user. **Bob** then submits this certificate to our user, **Robyn**. **Robyn** contacts the CA to validate the certificate and Bob's identity. The CA then verifies that the certificate from Bob is valid, so Robyn now trusts Bob.

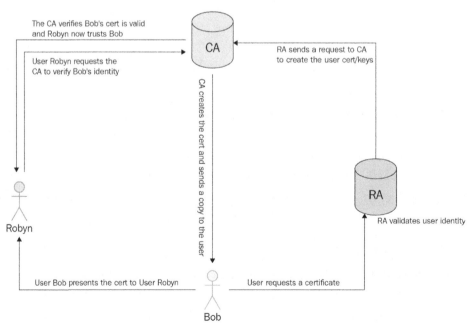

Figure 5.3 – PKI example

- **Can you describe quantum cryptography?**

  Quantum cryptography uses light particles (photons) to transmit data between locations over fiber optic cables. The sender of the data transmits the light particles through a polarizer that characterizes the particles with one of the four possible bit polarizations:

  - Horizontal (0-bit)

  - Vertical (1-bit)

  - 45 degrees left (0-bit)

  - 45 degrees right (1-bit)

  The particles then move to a receiver that uses two beam splitters to read the polarization of each particle. The receiver then notifies the sender which beam splitter was used for the particles in the sequence that was sent; the sender compares that information with the sequence of polarizers that was used to send the key and discards any photons that were read with the wrong beam splitter. The remaining sequence of bits becomes the key. This method helps protect data because if anyone eavesdrops on the communication and reads or attempts to copy the data, the state of the photon will change and be detected by the endpoint.

- **What is PGP?**

  Pretty good privacy (PGP) is a protocol that is used to encrypt and decrypt data. It provides authentication and cryptographic privacy. PGP is used to compress data, for digital signing, for the encryption and decryption of messages, emails, files, and directories, and to help improve the privacy of communication via email.

- **What is the difference between stream and block ciphers?**

  In block ciphers, the plaintext input is broken up into fixed-size blocks and the blocks are then encrypted and decrypted as a block.

  Examples of block ciphers include the DES and the AES.

  In stream ciphers, the plaintext input is encrypted and decrypted by an individual byte. An example of a stream cipher is **Rivest cipher 4 (RC4)**.

A fundamental understanding of symmetric and asymmetric cryptography is critical for cryptography roles, and you also need to be aware of emerging areas, such as quantum cryptography.

Summary

In this chapter, you learned about the cryptography career path and the average salary for this career in the United States. You also learned how working as a cryptographer can be a stepping stone into more advanced careers and learned some of the common interview questions that might be asked of you.

In the next chapter, you will learn about a career as a GRC analyst, including common knowledge-based interview questions you might be asked.

6
GRC/Privacy Analyst

This chapter focuses on **the governance, risk, and compliance (GRC)** analyst and privacy analyst roles. These roles are commonly overlooked as a cybersecurity role given their focus on policies and procedures rather than hands-on keyboard technical skills, but they are a great path into the world of cybersecurity and provide exposure to many different areas of the field.

The following topics will be covered in this chapter:

- What is a GRC/privacy analyst?
- How much can you make in this career?
- What other careers can this type of role lead to?
- What certifications should be considered?
- Common interview questions for a GRC/privacy analyst

What is a GRC/privacy analyst?

A GRC analyst is responsible for the assessment and documentation of an organization's policies and regulations associated with the compliance and risk posture of information assets. The overall goal of an individual in this role is to ensure alignment between technology decisions and business outcomes while working to continuously improve operational efficiencies. GRC analysts may function as part of an organization's internal security team or in more of a consultative capacity in which they would provide guidance to a company's internal security team as a representative of a third-party organization.

Specific responsibilities may include risk identification and analysis, policy development, auditing, reporting, and maintaining regulatory compliance. A privacy analyst role is similar to that of a GRC analyst from an activity and responsibility perspective. The difference, however, is that a privacy analyst, as the name implies, is specifically focused, ensuring that a company's business operations, policies, and procedures meet privacy requirements and regulations pertaining to the protection of critical information.

How much can you make in this career?

At the time of writing, the average annual salary for both GRC and privacy analyst falls within the range of $60,000 to $115,000. Salary influencers for this type of role are based on factors such as level of experience, specialization, industry, and location.

What other careers can this type of role lead to?

GRC/privacy analysts require a very broad perspective into corporate functions and processes. Although the role is not directly responsible for the management and deployment of technology, individuals in this role must possess a solid understanding of risk management and the technology used as mitigating controls, thereby making the possibilities endless.

In addition, GRC/privacy analysts can potentially be exposed to companies that span a broad range of industries, which, in turn, may lead to working with various laws and regulatory requirements, providing a path to focusing on a career as a security auditor (see *Chapter 7*, *Security Auditor*, for more details).

From a soft skills perspective, constant effective communication (both written and verbal) is required for this type of role due to interviewing and documentation requirements. This type of experience can help build confidence and the skills required to lead and manage teams.

What certifications should be considered?

To get started in the role of a GRC/privacy analyst, you can consider the following courses:

- **CompTIA Security+** helps establish a baseline of security knowledge when pursuing an information security/cybersecurity career. For more information, visit `https://www.comptia.org/certifications/security`.

- **CSA's Certificate of Cloud Security Knowledge (CCSK)** is similar to Security+ in that it is a vendor-agnostic, baseline-level exam with a specific focus on cloud security. For more information, visit `https://cloudsecurityalliance.org/education/ccsk/`.

- **ISACA's Certified Information Security Auditor (CISA)** is suited for professional and experienced auditing, monitoring, controlling, and assessing the business and IT systems of organizations. For more information, visit `https://www.isaca.org/credentialing/cisa?utm_source=google&utm_medium=cpc&utm_campaign=CertBAU&utm_content=sem_CertBAU_certification-cisa-na-exam-google&cid=sem_2006830&Appeal=sem&gclid=Cj0KCQiAraSPBhDuARIsAM3Js4qgEODANZqgpbLCevK4RamBq_e0aTSNQdX5No0JnnmSpkJ2V_B8Lm0aAjhbEALw_wcB`.

- **ISACA's Certified Information Security Manager (CISM)** validates expertise in areas such as security program governance, development, and management, as well as incident and risk management. For more information, visit `https://www.isaca.org/credentialing/cism?utm_source=google&utm_medium=cpc&utm_campaign=CertBAU&utm_content=sem_CertBAU_certification-cism-na-product-google&cid=sem_2006855&Appeal=sem&gclid=Cj0KCQiAraSPBhDuARIsAM3Js4ro26VfkP8QA_RtNFpyYUAeKM1yyAdOGivCHGy9g9uCfNvPWaRXlTEaAreFEALw_wcB`.

Next, let's look at a few interview questions that will help you with your interview.

Common interview questions for a GRC/ privacy analyst

As a GRC/privacy analyst, it is important to understand common frameworks, standards, and regulations relative to the industry vertical of the company being pursued as an employer. For example, knowledge of the **Health Insurance Portability and Accountability Act (HIPAA)** would be necessary for an analyst pursuing a career in the healthcare industry, while **Sarbanes-Oxley (SOX)** would be more suited for an analyst headed down the path of finance.

The following is a list of interview questions that could prove useful in preparing for a GRC/privacy analyst interview:

- **What is GRC and why is it important to an organization?**

  Seems like a silly question, right?! Well, has anyone ever asked you your age and you had to stop and think about it for a moment? Yeah, you don't want that to happen to you in an interview. A very simple question, and sure, you know exactly what it is in your mind, but have you practiced articulating it verbally?

  Let's start with the easy part. GRC is a strategy used by organizations to manage **governance** (ensuring IT processes align with business goals), **risk** (events or situations that could be damaging to the organization), and **compliance** (meeting legal and regulatory requirements). GRC is critically important to a company's success and sustainability as it directly impacts an organization's ability to achieve its goals and align with the desired outcomes of stakeholders.

  Benefits include the following:

  - It improves activities associated with managing, identifying, and evaluating risk.

  - It aids in strategic planning related to policy and corporate management activities.

  - It focuses on adherence to legal and regulatory compliance requirements.

  Now, let's dig a bit more into risk management.

Risk management

The purpose of risk management is to inform the development of strategic security initiatives aimed at identifying and evaluating organizational risk and then reduce the risk to an acceptable level. Sources of corporate risk are not limited to technology, however. When assessing organizational risk, it is essential to consider all aspects of risk (logical, physical, internal, external, and so on), so that the organization is not vulnerable due to blind spots. For example, when evaluating a manufacturer's organizational risk, analysts should consider intellectual property and data privacy in addition to critical infrastructure.

After identifying and evaluating the risk posed to an organization, a decision will need to be made regarding the appropriate action to take in response; this informs the risk mitigation strategy. The four most commonly exercised risk responses are as follows:

- **Risk acceptance** – When a risk is accepted, security leaders and business decision makers have agreed to own the consequences and loss associated with a risk that is realized. A company may elect to accept an identified risk because the cost associated with the loss does not outweigh the countermeasure cost, for example.

- **Risk transfer** – Companies transfer risk by assigning ownership of the cost of a loss to a separate entity. Examples of this include purchasing cybersecurity insurance and outsourcing.

- **Risk avoidance** – Avoiding risk involves replacing the risk with a less risky alternative or removing it altogether. An example of this is building a data center in a location other than Florida to avoid hurricanes. Another example is avoiding **File Transfer Protocol (FTP)** attacks by disabling the FTP protocol across the organization.

- **Risk reduction/mitigation** – Implementing controls and countermeasures to protect the organization from threats and eradicate vulnerabilities is the goal of risk reduction. The approach should be cost-effective and based on the cost/benefit analysis performed during risk identification and evaluation.

Cybersecurity approaches

The risk management process should lead to risk-reducing outcomes, which aligns with the need to communicate security program effectiveness in risk-reducing terms. Security teams find it increasingly difficult to identify, monitor, and measure organizational risk due to complex architecture, a lack of standardized information system policies, and the uncertainties of unknown security threats and unpredictable user behavior.

Maturity-based and cyber risk-based (or threat-focused) are the two most common approaches to cybersecurity. While both processes offer the ability to monitor and measure program effectiveness, they produce very distinct outcomes.

Maturity-based approach

Maturity-based programs focus on building defined capabilities to achieve a desired level of maturity. Although the technique is not explicitly targeting risk reduction as an outcome, it is still considered the industry norm for cyber risk management. While organizations seeking to establish an operation have seen success with this approach, as the model matures, the constant requirement to monitor and improve all program capabilities often results in inefficient spending and unmanageable tool sprawl.

Cyber risk-based approach

A cyber risk-based focus positions companies to identify the most significant vulnerabilities and threats and implement countermeasures to reduce the most critical organizational cyber risks. Following this path allows security teams to prioritize program investments (driving cost-effective decisions) and articulate risk-reducing outcomes. Many industry experts argue that when compared to the maturity-based approach, it is, in fact, the cyber risk-based operating model that is better suited to help security teams keep pace with the evolving threat landscape due to its flexibility and specificity. However, the inherent challenge for security teams when leveraging this approach is the lack of well-defined metrics due to the wide range of actions companies may choose to prioritize.

Finally, we will dive into frameworks.

Frameworks

In general, frameworks exist to enable business leaders and professionals to communicate in a common language, leveraging a defined set of standards. Similarly, cybersecurity frameworks aid security leaders in securing digital assets by providing a reliable and logical process for reducing cyber risk. It is important to note that there are three types of security frameworks:

- **Control frameworks** offer guidance on assessing the state of an organization's technical controls, establishing a baseline of technical controls deemed appropriate for the business, and prioritizing implementation. A widely used control framework is the Center for Internet Security's Critical Security Controls. The following is a list of the CIS controls in v8, and how many safeguards in each apply to each of the control implementation groups:

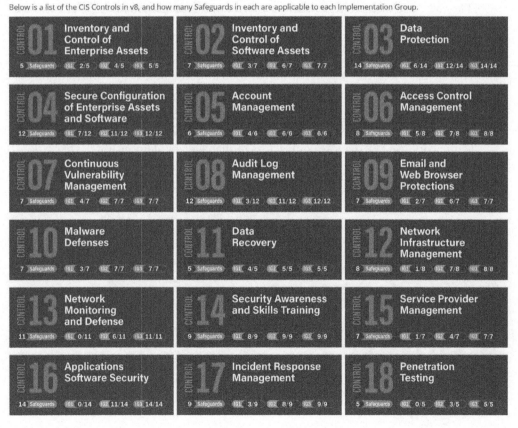

Below is a list of the CIS Controls in v8, and how many Safeguards in each are applicable to each Implementation Group.

CONTROL 01	Inventory and Control of Enterprise Assets	CONTROL 02	Inventory and Control of Software Assets	CONTROL 03	Data Protection
5 Safeguards IG1 2/5 IG2 4/5 IG3 5/5		7 Safeguards IG1 3/7 IG2 6/7 IG3 7/7		14 Safeguards IG1 6/14 IG2 12/14 IG3 14/14	
CONTROL 04	Secure Configuration of Enterprise Assets and Software	CONTROL 05	Account Management	CONTROL 06	Access Control Management
12 Safeguards IG1 7/12 IG2 11/12 IG3 12/12		6 Safeguards IG1 4/6 IG2 6/6 IG3 6/6		8 Safeguards IG1 5/8 IG2 7/8 IG3 8/8	
CONTROL 07	Continuous Vulnerability Management	CONTROL 08	Audit Log Management	CONTROL 09	Email and Web Browser Protections
7 Safeguards IG1 4/7 IG2 7/7 IG3 7/7		12 Safeguards IG1 3/12 IG2 11/12 IG3 12/12		7 Safeguards IG1 2/7 IG2 6/7 IG3 7/7	
CONTROL 10	Malware Defenses	CONTROL 11	Data Recovery	CONTROL 12	Network Infrastructure Management
7 Safeguards IG1 3/7 IG2 7/7 IG3 7/7		5 Safeguards IG1 4/5 IG2 5/5 IG3 5/5		8 Safeguards IG1 1/8 IG2 7/8 IG3 8/8	
CONTROL 13	Network Monitoring and Defense	CONTROL 14	Security Awareness and Skills Training	CONTROL 15	Service Provider Management
11 Safeguards IG1 0/11 IG2 6/11 IG3 11/11		9 Safeguards IG1 8/9 IG2 9/9 IG3 9/9		7 Safeguards IG1 1/7 IG2 4/7 IG3 7/7	
CONTROL 16	Applications Software Security	CONTROL 17	Incident Response Management	CONTROL 18	Penetration Testing
14 Safeguards IG1 0/14 IG2 11/14 IG3 14/14		9 Safeguards IG1 3/9 IG2 8/9 IG3 9/9		5 Safeguards IG1 0/5 IG2 3/5 IG3 5/5	

Figure 6.1 – CIS controls in v8 (Source: https://www.cisecurity.org/controls)

- **Program frameworks** provide a process for assessing, building, and measuring an organization's security program. An example of a program framework is the **National Institute of Standards and Technology (NIST)** framework for improving critical infrastructure cybersecurity (NIST Cybersecurity Framework). The following diagram shows version 1.1 of the NIST CSF:

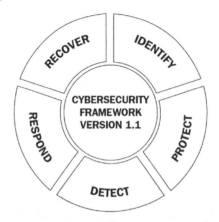

Figure 6.2 – NIST Cybersecurity Framework 1.1

- **Risk frameworks** offer a structured approach to managing cyber risk by identifying, measuring, and quantifying risk, and then prioritizing mitigation activities. The NIST **Risk Management Framework (RMF)** is a common framework used by defense contractors to manage and demonstrate cyber risk mitigation activities and security posture improvements. The following diagram is a snapshot of the NIST RMF and the definitions of each of the stages:

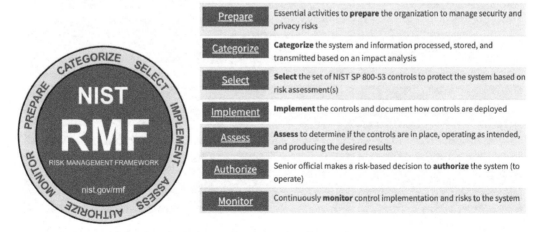

Figure 6.3 – NIST Risk Management Framework (Source: `https://csrc.nist.gov/Projects/risk-management`)

- **How does preventive control differ from detective control?**

As the names imply, the purpose of preventive control is to actively prevent a threat, while detective control will only detect a threat. You might ask yourself why an organization would want to use a control only capable of detecting, but not capable of taking any action, and that's a great question. It really boils down to taking a layered or defense-in-depth approach to security and using the right tool for the job.

For example, consider modern-day **endpoint protection** (**EPP**), which typically offers a combination of a **next-generation antivirus** (**NGAV**) and **endpoint detection and response** (**EDR**). Together, they are incredibly powerful because the NGAV will prevent malicious activity, and the EDR records all of the process-level activity so that in the event a threat can bypass the NGAV, the activity can still be detected, and detailed forensics are available to assist in determining the appropriate response action. The following diagram aligns the different control types to their place in the life cycle of a cyber attack:

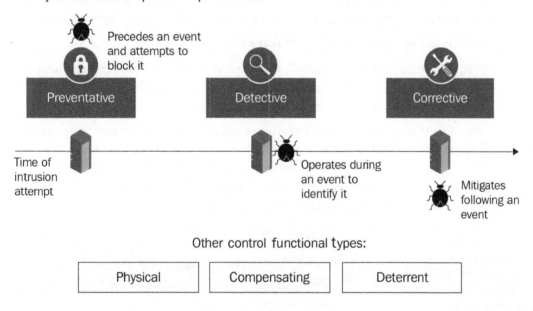

Figure 6.4 – Control types

- **Describe how GRC risk management is used.**

GRC risk management aims to identify, classify, and quantify organizational risk. As part of the process, the appropriate risk responses (avoid, mitigate, accept, transfer) are determined and, in the case of mitigation, preventive and detective mitigation control methods are performed.

- **What makes a successful GRC/privacy analyst?**

  In addition to understanding the necessary framework, methodologies, regulatory requirements, and more, successful GRC/privacy analysts are able to build relationships and communicate with a broad range of teams possessing varying levels of technical and business acumen. The analyst must be able to serve as a bridge and interpreter between cross-functional teams and different organizational units.

- **Provide an example of a risk management framework.**

  A popular and widely adopted risk management framework is NIST RMF (`https://csrc.nist.gov/projects/risk-management/about-rmf`). According to NIST, the framework provides a method for integrating security, privacy, and cyber supply chain risk management activities into the system development life cycle. The goal of the framework is to aid in selecting and integrating security controls in a risk-based fashion. The steps of the framework are as follows: Prepare, Categorize, Select, Implement, Assess, Authorize, and Monitor.

- **What is the difference between a threat and a vulnerability?**

  In short, a vulnerability represents a weakness in an organization's environment. This weakness can exist in software, hardware, and even in processes. A threat, on the other hand, is anything that can exploit a vulnerability.

  The terms threat, vulnerability, and risk are often confused, so be sure you're clear on each term as a standalone entity, as well as in relation to one another. We've already touched on threat and vulnerability, but it's also good to know that within the context of this question, risk is defined as the potential for damage, or the loss of data, or the destruction of assets caused by a threat.

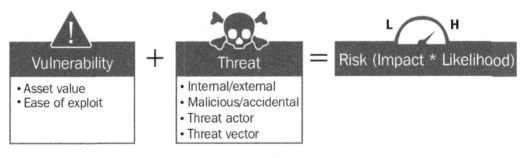

Figure 6.5 – Risk formula

- **How should a risk be classified?**

  This question can be a trap. The answer is very simple, but in the right moment, could lead a candidate down a long and dark path of overexplaining. The very simple answer is that while risk should ultimately be classified according to priority (critical, high, medium, and low), the specifics of the classifications should align with company policy.

- **Define and provide examples of risk response within the context of risk management.**

  When managing an organization's cybersecurity risk, the overall outcome is to determine a cost-effective solution for reducing or mitigating the risk to a level that is acceptable according to the organization's priorities and tolerance levels. The four most common responses are as follows:

  - **Accept** – This typically means the cost of mitigation outweighs the cost of risk realization.

  - **Mitigate/reduce** – Implement controls to reduce the risk to a level that is within the organization's tolerance level.

  - **Transfer** – Make it someone else's problem (in other words, cybersecurity insurance).

  - **Avoid** – The process or solution being assessed is rejected because it is not worth the risk it poses to the organization.

- **What is GDPR and when does it apply?**

  GDPR stands for **General Data Protection Regulation** and is viewed as the toughest privacy and security law in the world. The effective date of the regulation was May 25, 2018, and although it was drafted and passed by the **European Union (EU)**, its impact is global.

  The regulation is intended to protect the privacy and security of data and targets any organization that handles data related to people in the EU.

- **What is the ARR?**

  ARR stands for **audit risk rating** and is used to establish the criteria to be leveraged by an organization for risk rating and ranking.

- **What is the difference between security and privacy?**

  Although the two are very closely related, they are not one and the same. Privacy refers to an individual's right to control the use of their personal information, whereas security refers to how information is protected; use versus protection. There is a clear overlap between the two, but they are still two separate and very important considerations. The following scenario illustrates a few examples of the differences.

  Scenario: You walk into a car dealership and purchase a car. The dealer collects your personal information and stores your payment details for future use. What's the worst that could happen? Let's take a look…

  - The dealer uses your personal information to open a loan with the bank to cover the cost of your vehicle. They charge the card you left on file $2,500 to cover the down payment. Your data is stored on a secure server and only accessible by individuals who require access to perform their daily job. **Outcome**: *Your information is secure, and your privacy is maintained.*

  - You signed a bunch of paperwork when you were there and one of the documents was the dealer's privacy disclosure. The dealer sells your information to an agency that provides marketing services to major auto insurance companies. **Outcome**: *Your information is still secure, but your privacy is now compromised.*

  - The dealership is breached, and attackers steal the account details of everyone that has ever considered purchasing a car from this location since its doors first opened 15 years ago. **Outcome**: *The security and the privacy of your data are compromised.*

- **What privacy laws are you familiar with and what industries are they applicable to?**

  These laws include the following:

  - **HIPAA (Health Insurance Portability and Accountability Act of 1996)** – This is the standard that governs the protection of **patient health information (PHI)** and applies to the healthcare industry.

  - **FERPA (Family Educational Rights and Privacy Act)** – This is a federal law applicable to all schools receiving funds through a US Department of Education program. The law protects the privacy of student education records.

  - **GDPR (General Data Protection Regulation)** – Protects the privacy and security of data of people in the EU. It does not apply to a specific industry. The regulation has a very broad reach and applies to any organization in any industry that handles data related to people in the EU.

Also of note, three states have introduced consumer data privacy laws:

- **California's Consumer Privacy Act of 2018 (CCPA)**

- Colorado's Privacy Act (which was created within its Consumer Protection Act)

- Virginia's Consumer Data Protection Act

At a high level, the laws are in place to provide consumers with the right to access, delete, update, and/or obtain a copy of their personal data. There are some slight differences within the laws, so it would be worthwhile having a solid understanding of any and all laws that apply to your potential employer.

Additional details on these and other key consumer privacy laws can be found on the **NCSL (National Conference of State Legislatures)**'s website: `https://www.ncsl.org/`.

- **What is CIA and why is it important?**

  CIA in the context of cybersecurity refers to the confidentially, integrity, and availability of data and systems. The CIA triad serves as the foundation- or base-level principle for development security policies and systems. The focus of confidentially is to ensure that data can only be viewed by authorized entities. The goal of integrity is to ensure that data remains tamper-free and trustworthy. Integrity is lost if data is not authentic, accurate, and reliable. If data is inaccessible, the importance of confidentiality and integrity diminishes somewhat. Availability efforts are aimed at ensuring that data, applications, systems, networks, and so on are available and function properly.

- **Explain how encryption can be leveraged to ensure data privacy.**

  Data privacy refers to an individual's right to control the use of their personal information. Encryption makes this possible by scrambling plain text into an unreadable format with an encryption key. This hides the data from potential eavesdroppers because only the person or entity with the decryption key can convert the unreadable data back into plain text.

- **How does technical control differ from administrative control?**

  Simply put, technical control is a tool (firewall, IDS/IPS, antivirus, and so on), whereas administrative control is a policy (data classification, employee onboarding/offboarding, acceptable use, and more).

The preceding questions are intended to offer insights into the types of questions you might be asked in an interview for a role as a GRC/privacy analyst. You should now have a better understanding of how to narrow your focus in preparation for interviews of this type.

An important tip to remember: it is not enough to simply understand the history and key points within laws and regulations. It is also important to understand the problem being solved in addition to the potential business impact and implications. This will vary from organization to organization, as well as from industry to industry.

Lastly, a great way to differentiate yourself in an interview is to be aware and well informed of upcoming changes to laws and regulations, especially those that directly impact the organization that has called you in for an interview. For example, the CPRA expands California's consumer data privacy laws and is set to take effect on January 1, 2023.

Summary

In this chapter, you learned what a GRC/privacy analyst is and what the average salaries are in the United States for roles of this type, along with certification considerations, career path options, and common questions you might be asked during an interview. While understanding the questions and answers as stated is important, be sure to explore beyond the specifics in the questions themselves to ensure you understand the surrounding concepts.

In the next chapter, we will learn about a career as a security auditor.

7
Security Auditor

In this chapter, you will learn what a security auditor is and the average salary range for this career in the US. You will also learn about the career progression options and common interview questions for the role.

The following topics will be covered in this chapter:

- What is a security auditor?
- How much can you make in this career?
- What other careers can you do?
- Common interview questions for a security auditor career

What is a security auditor?

A **security auditor** is an individual who helps to provide an independent systematic review of an organization's information security system. Sometimes they work as individuals. Other times, they can perform as part of a team or department providing audit services inside an organization. Security auditors can also be external consultants that provide an independent systematic review of their client's information security system or scoped parts of it per their contract.

Security auditors conduct their audits based on the organizational policies and any applicable government compliance and regulations. They work with **information technology (IT)** personnel, security, managers, executives, and other business stakeholders to validate the business's industry best practices versus any applicable policy regulation or best practice. Auditors achieve this by using questionnaires, interviews, monitoring their work, samples of past work, or validation that controls and procedures work the way they are expected to work.

How much can you make in this career?

The salary range of a security auditor ranges from $60,000 to $120,000. It can be higher or lower depending on the location of the candidate, years of experience, and demand for the other areas of specialization that they might have, for example, cloud security or application security experience.

What other careers can you do?

Having a career as a security auditor prepares you for various other occupations. The combination of experiences you gain as a security auditor allows you to gain the expertise needed to provide consulting engagements. For example, as a security auditor, you regularly look at best practices and make recommendations for testing and control programs. Security auditors often go on to help lead **governance, risk, and compliance (GRC)** programs for organizations, using their auditor experience to highlight and remediate deficiencies in making laws and regulations and internal requirements. Another potentially exciting career pivot for an auditor would be as a penetration and vulnerability tester.

Other subspecialties include secure software assessor or security control assessor, which might be more prominent in the government or government contractor space.

Common interview questions

The following is a list of interview questions that could prove useful in preparing for a security auditor interview:

- **What frameworks are you familiar with or have you performed assessments against?**

  In addition to the internal policies and procedures of the hiring company, auditors will need to be familiar with federal regulations such as the **Health Insurance Portability and Accountability Act (HIPAA)** (`https://www.cdc.gov/phlp/publications/topic/hipaa.html`) and **Sarbanes-Oxley Act (SOX)** (`https://www.law.cornell.edu/wex/sarbanes-oxley_act`), or standards set by the **International Organization for Standardization (ISO)** (`https://www.iso.org/isoiec-27001-information-security.html`) or the **National Institute for Standards in Technology (NIST)** (`https://www.nist.gov/`).

- **What are the standard certifications that a security auditor might have?**

  Some of the standard certifications that a security auditor might have are as follows:

  - **Certified Information Systems Auditor (CISA)** from ISACA (`https://www.isaca.org/credentialing/cisa`). CRISC is helpful for those focusing on risk and system controls.

  - **CompTIA Security+** from CompTIA (`https://www.comptia.org/certifications/security`). CySA+ is another helpful certification from this provider.

  - **IT Infrastructure Library (ITIL)** certification (`https://niccs.cisa.gov/training/search/standard-technology-incorporated/it-infrastructure-library-itil-foundation`).

  - Certifications for specific **cloud service providers (CSPs)** or systems providers.

  While there are a host of other certification providers and certificates, I would recommend that you consider how a specific certificate is focused on your career and its trajectory.

- **What are the differences between general controls and system and application controls?**

  As an organization develops its internal policies and guidelines, they form the basis of general controls to which all the people and processes must adhere. Controls then become more granular at the system level; this can be at the CSP level or the virtual machine or operating system layer. To achieve even more granularity, each system might have specific controls to ensure that the internal policies and procedures are met.

- **How would you approach an audit for an organization?**

  When coming into a new organization for an audit engagement, the lead must schedule a meeting with all the stakeholders to define the audit objectives and understand the organization's context. Work with the stakeholders to develop a preliminary schedule for the audit and all the potential individuals involved. Create a specific budget (even if you are not responsible for the financials, budget in time using hours) and define the scope of the engagement. Then, based on the budget or time and scope, you will list the audit team members, specify tasks for each individual, and determine the deadlines.

  With the plan in place, you will start the audit. An audit generally has the following eight phases:

  1. Risk assessment
  2. Audit plan
  3. Preliminary review
  4. Design audit procedures
  5. Test controls
  6. Substantive testing
  7. Document results
  8. Communications

  More information on assessments and auditing can be found at `https://www.nist.gov/cyberframework/assessment-auditing-resources`. When working with or for the government, it is essential to follow the NIST RMF (`https://csrc.nist.gov/projects/risk-management`) and the federal controls (`https://csrc.nist.gov/Projects/risk-management/sp800-53-controls/release-search#!/800-53?version=4.0`).

- **Can you name some of the different types of audits?**

  Some different types of audits are information system audits, compliance audits, financial audits, operational audits, integrated audits, specialized audits, computer forensic audits, and functional audits:

  - **Information system (IS)** audits are used to determine whether ISs and their related infrastructure are protected to maintain confidentiality, integrity, and availability.

  - **Compliance audits** are used to determine whether specific regulatory requirements are being complied with.

  - **Financial audits** are used to determine the accuracy of financial reports.

  - **Operational audits** are used to determine the accuracy of internal control systems and help identify issues related to the efficiency of operational productivity within the organization.

  - **Integrated audits** can be performed by internal or external auditors and are a blend of the other audit types used to assess the overall efficiency and compliance of an asset.

  - **Specialized audits** can include fraud audits, forensic audits, and third-party service audits.

  - **Computer forensic audits** are used to ensure compliance with the system during an investigation.

  - **Functional audits** are conducted prior to the implementation of new software to determine whether the software is functioning accurately.

- **What does the audit charter typically include?**

  The audit charter normally includes the purpose and objective of the audit team, the audit team's scope, the team members, and the responsibilities of each team member.

- **What are some of the risks associated with point of sale (POS)?**

  Some of the risks include skimming and the unauthorized disclosure of PINs.

- **During an e-commerce IS audit, what are some of the responsibilities of the auditor?**

  An auditor should review the overall security architecture, review the continuous monitoring and alerting processes of the organization for e-commerce transactions, review the organization's incident management program, review business **service-level agreements (SLAs)** for business continuity, and review security controls for privacy.

- **Can you describe the phases of an audit?**

  There are three main phases to an audit, which are the planning phase, the execution phase, and the reporting phase:

  - The **planning phase** contains the following steps:

    1. Risk assessment and determining the physical location that will be audited
    2. Determining the objective of the audit
    3. Determining the scope of the audit
    4. Pre-audit planning
    5. Determining the audit procedures that will be followed

  - The **execution phase** contains the following steps:

    1. Gathering relevant data and documents to conduct the audit
    2. Evaluating existing controls to determine their effectiveness and efficiency
    3. Validating and documenting your observations during the audit and providing evidence

  - The **reporting phase** contains the following steps:

    1. Creating a draft report and discussing it with management Alignment
    2. Issuing a final audit report that contains the findings of the audit, evidence, recommendations, comments from management, and the expected date of closure of the audit findings
    3. Conducting a follow-up to determine whether the audit findings are now closed and issuing a follow-up report

- **What outlines the overall authority to conduct an IS audit?**

  The audit charter outlines the overall authority to conduct an IS audit and it also includes the objectives of the audit and the audit's responsibility.

- **Describe the difference between a vulnerability and a threat.**

  A vulnerability is a weakness in a system, which could be insecure code, weak security controls implemented, or a human factor. A threat is something that exploits this weakness, so this could be criminal hackers, ransomware or other malware, or something else such as a hurricane.

- **Describe the term "assumed breach."**

  As technology systems (hardware/software) are created by humans, and humans are subject to error, we can assume that a particular system might have some vulnerability to it. If we can all agree on that assumption, we should also all agree that there is the potential that your systems have already been breached. This means that, as part of daily operations, you are ensuring that all secrets are protected, identities are verified to only be granted the needed access, and that you are looking for potential **indicators of compromise (IOCs)** or **indicators of attack (IOAs)**. In this type of environment, there is little to zero inherited trust between people and systems. An example of an IOC is a workstation doing a callout to an unknown IP address, and an example of an IOA could be a PowerShell script being run on a user workstation where that user typically would not be running PowerShell scripts.

- **What is the difference between residual and inherent risk?**

  Inherent risk is the risk before any security controls are applied. This concept is often hard to understand for some, especially as there are so many controls that might come into play before a particular application or risk situation. It is important to talk through the nuances of this with your stakeholders before proceeding with the impending risk-based conversation.

  Residual risk is the risk left over after applying security controls. Once you have arrived at this stage, it is important to consider the likelihood/frequency of the risk situations and the varying levels of potential impact when thinking about the residual risk and trying to quantify it.

- **What are the common steps in conducting a risk-based audit?**

  The steps in a risk-based audit are as follows:

  1. The first step is to obtain the pre-audit requirements, which include knowledge of the client's industry and regulatory requirements, knowledge of applicable risks to the client, and knowledge from prior audits.

  2. The second step is to gain knowledge about the internal security controls in use, which includes knowledge of the client's control environment and procedures, understanding the risks of the controls, and understanding detection risks.

3. The next step is to conduct compliance testing, which includes identifying the security controls to be tested and determining their effectiveness.

4. The last step is to conduct a substantive test and ensure that it includes appropriate analytical procedures and detailed testing of account balances and procedures.

- **What do you do if your client fails to implement the recommendations you made in your audit report?**

The most important thing to do is relate your audit findings to real-world examples showing how correcting the issue can help the team and organization. For example, a manager of a department may ignore your audit findings because they don't see the value and think of correcting the issue as a burden on their already-reduced available time and budget. Showing them how another department implemented changes that helped reduce cost and/or improved productivity can help. The other thing you should do is ensure you are providing the process to the client for how you suggest they fix the issue. As an example, if your audit discovers that employee user accounts were not properly terminated when the employees left, the client might just remove those accounts. This does not fix the problem for the client in the future when other employees are terminated. Instead, recommend the client implements a process for identifying when employees leave the organization and how user account access is then removed.

- **When should you recommend the use of compensating security controls?**

Compensating security controls are alternate security controls that organizations can use to fulfill a compliance standard, such as the **Payment Card Industry Data Security Standard (PCI DSS)** (`https://www.pcisecuritystandards.org/pci_security/`).

The alternate security controls must meet the intent and the same level of rigor as the original compliance requirement, provide an equivalent level of defense, and be comparable in the level of risk.

Compensating security controls are typically used when the organization has some type of constraint that prevents the implementation of the original security control in the compliance standard.

An example of compensating security controls would be a small company that does not have enough staff in their financial department to have two or more people complete separate parts of a task. In this case, the small company might just use monitoring and analysis of logs and audit trails to track suspicious behavior in financial transactions.

- **What are some of the risks associated with using third-party security services?**

A third party could be compromised to launch a cyber attack against the client's organization, such as in the Target data breach (`https://www.nbcnews.com/business/business-news/target-settles-2013-hacked-customer-data-breach-18-5-million-n764031`). The third party may also limit the visibility of the client into logs and auditing data that might be required for the client to maintain compliance.

Having an effective mechanism for ensuring that your third parties are prioritized based on risk and that the level of controls in place are also based on that risk will lead to a great risk-informed third-party management program.

- **What are some of the challenges when working with an environment that is based in the cloud or has a hybrid cloud/on-premises approach?**

As a security auditor, your role is often to ensure that an organization has the right controls in place or that the controls in place are functioning in an effective manner as intended. Where controls tend to have a blurred line is when it comes to working in a third-party environment such as a CSP. When working with a CSP, there is often a reliance on them to implement certain controls and you would inherit them from the CSP in your controls catalog. For example, when working with a CSP, you are no longer responsible for things such as the physical safety, power requirements, and physical maintenance of the machines, so if you have controls like that for your own physical environment, they would be inherited from the CSP.

Here is an example of the AWS shared responsibility model so that you can see which type of controls might have a customer or AWS responsibility:

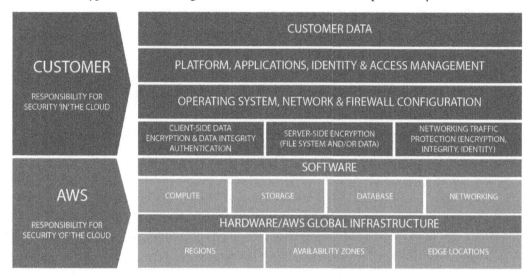

Figure 7.1 – AWS shared responsibility model

Here is the Azure shared responsibility model:

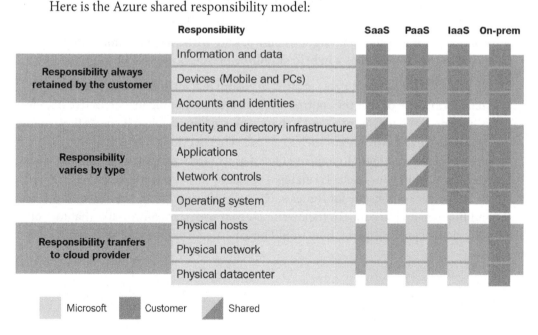

Figure 7.2 – Microsoft Azure shared responsibility model

Here is an example of the shared responsibility model from **Google Cloud Platform (GCP)**:

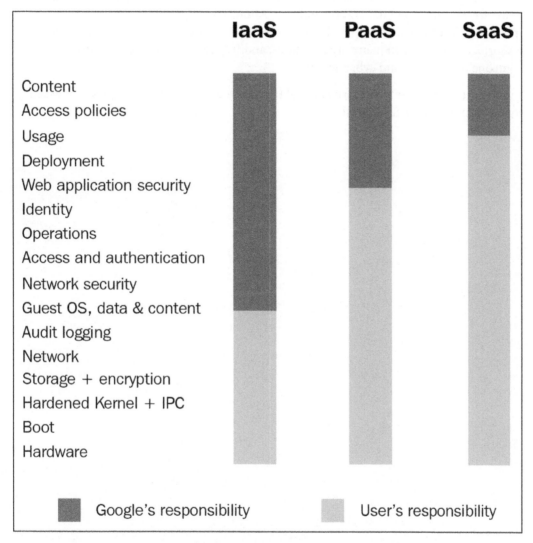

Figure 7.3 – Google Cloud Platform shared responsibility model

As you can see, where the shared responsibility line is drawn is slightly different depending on the CSP, and it is your job to ensure that the organization is considering the right controls and that they are functioning effectively.

During an interview, you may experience a broad set of questions about auditing. Use the questions in this section as a guide and also provide examples to the interviewer using your real-life experience with clients.

Summary

In this chapter, you learned what a security auditor is, the average salaries in the United States for a security auditor, and common questions you might be asked during an interview. Careers in auditing can be rewarding and lucrative, and since there is typically a shortage of auditors in many organizations, auditing can be a good career selection for someone newer to IT and cybersecurity.

In the next chapter, you will learn some of the most common interview questions asked for a career as a malware analyst.

8
Malware Analyst

In this chapter, you will learn what a malware analyst is and the average salary range for this career in the US. You will also learn about the career progression options and some common interview questions for the role. This career is typically for someone with experience already in another cybersecurity role, such as a SOC analyst, and not typically a career path for entry-level individuals. It's important to note that some of the questions listed in this chapter will require you to have background knowledge of assembly language. If you do not have this background knowledge, please be prepared to conduct additional research on the topics in the questions using educational materials (such as books, online courses, blog articles, and podcasts) that work best for your learning style.

The following topics will be covered in this chapter:

- What is a malware analyst?
- How much can you make in this career?
- What other careers can you do?
- Common interview questions for a malware analyst career

What is a malware analyst?

Malware analysts analyze different types of malware to understand the threat. This can include identifying the capabilities of the malware, how the malware functions, and identifying **indicators of compromise** (**IOCs**) that can be used to identify the malware. Other job titles you may see include malware reverse engineer. A solid background in programming, networking, system administration, and operating systems is helpful for malware analyst roles. Malware analysts also need to stay current on the latest threats. It is extremely helpful to have some knowledge of assembly as you progress in your malware analyst career.

There are typically two types of malware analysts:

- **Escalation malware analysts** work with **incident response** (**IR**) teams and analyze malware samples to determine the functionality of the malware, what it might have done on the system, and artifacts (for example, URLs, filenames, and hashes) that will help the IR team look for the infection on other systems.

- **Collection malware analysts** usually work for a security company and go through public and private feeds to identify IOCs that can be ingested by security appliances to help the security company's customers identify and stop threats faster. As a collection malware analyst, you will typically specialize in a particular malware family and automate as much of the analysis process as possible for scalability.

The skills needed to be a malware analyst include curiosity, research skills, dynamic analysis (observing the malware behavior), static analysis (understanding properties of the file), and being able to articulate your process for analyzing a malware sample.

Malware Unicorn has a free introductory course on malware analysis: `https://malwareunicorn.org/workshops/re101.html#0`.

Open Analysis Labs has a good YouTube channel for learning about malware analysis: `https://www.youtube.com/c/OALabs`.

And, here is a free Malware Analysis Bootcamp on YouTube from HackerSploit: `https://youtu.be/BjRMbe0-kLI`.

How much can you make in this career?

The salary for a malware analyst can range from $82,000 to $187,000 or more, depending on your location, the company you work for, and your experience.

What other careers can you do?

A career as a malware analyst can lead to more senior roles such as a staff researcher and security researcher, where you will be hunting future trends of malware. You can also use your malware analysis skills to move into full-time digital forensics roles and work with law enforcement agencies.

Common interview questions for a malware analyst career

The following questions include a heavier focus on the analysis of PE headers and questions around assembly language. From my own experience in interviews, the majority of questions I received for malware analyst positions were around PE headers:

- **Can you name the common headers in a Portable Executable (PE) file?**

   The headers are the DOS header (`struct_IMAGE_DOS_HEADER`), NT header (`struct_IMAGE_NT_HEADER`), the file and optional headers that live within the NT header (`struct__IMAGE_FILE_HEADER` and `struct__IMAGE_OPTIONAL_HEADER` respectively), and the individual section headers (`struct_IMAGE_SECTION_HEADER`).

   When opening an executable in a hex editor, the DOS header will occupy the first four rows (64 bits) in the hex editor and also include MZ in the magic number field.

   The file header contains basic information about the file's layout and contains the following fields:

Starting Byte	Type	Information
1	WORD	Machine
3	WORD	Number of sections
5	DWORD	Time date stamp
9	DWORD	Pointer to symbol table
13	DWORD	Number of symbols
17	WORD	Size of optional header
19	WORD	Characteristics

Table 8.1 – Header fields

The optional header contains the `magic` field, `AddressofEntryPoint`, the `BaseOfCode` and `BaseOfData` fields, the `ImageBase` field, the `SectionAlignment` and `FileAlignment` fields, the `SizeOfImage` field, and the `Subsystem` field.

The `magic` field identifies whether the executable is 32-bit or 64-bit. The `AddressOfEntryPoint` field is the address where the Windows loader begins the execution, and it contains the **relative virtual address (RVA)** of the **entry point (EP)** of the module. The `BaseofCode` field contains the RVA of the start of the code section, and the `BaseofData` field contains the RVA of the start of the data section. The `ImageBase` field is where the executable is mapped to a specific location in memory. The `SectionAlignment` and `FileAlignment` fields are indicative of the alignment between the file and the memory locations. The `SizeOfImage` field contains the memory size that is occupied by the executable at runtime. The `Subsystem` field identifies the target subsystem for the executable file.

The individual section headers are contained in the section header table, which contains the `SizeOfRawData` field, the `VirtualSize` field, the `PointerToRawData` field, the `VirtualAddress` field, and the `Characteristics` field.

The `SizeOfRawData` field contains the information on the real size of the section within the executable. The `VirtualSize` field contains the size of the section in memory. The `PointerToRawData` field contains information about the offset where the section begins. The `VirtualAddress` field contains the RVA of each section in memory, and the `Characteristics` field displays the memory access rights for each section.

The most common section names are `.text`, `.data`, `.idata` or `.rdata`, `.reloc`, `.rsrc`, and `.debug`.

- **What is the difference between static and dynamic malware analysis?**

In **static malware analysis**, you collect information about a malware sample without executing the malware to determine whether there are indicators present that the file might be malicious. This could include analyzing the hash of the file against malware signature databases, checking for suspicious strings such as suspicious domains and IP addresses, and identifying whether the file is packed.

Dynamic malware analysis allows you to analyze the behavior of the suspicious file to determine whether it is malicious. You should conduct this analysis in a sandbox environment. You can build your own sandbox environment using **virtual machines** (**VMs**) and there are also online sandboxes. **AnyRun** is one example of an online malware sandbox that executes your file and provides reporting on suspicious behavior, along with information about whether the sample matches any known malware. You can run a free scan at their website: `https://any.run/`.

As a malware analyst, you will typically use a hybrid approach for analyzing malware, where you begin with your static analysis and then analyze the behavior of the sample.

- **What is process injection?**

Process injection is a technique used by threat actors to evade security tools and escalate privileges. Fundamentally, process injection is when the threat actor's code is run within an existing process. This allows the threat actor access to the existing process' network resources and memory and possibly allows for escalated privileges for the malicious code.

You can read more about process injection on the MITRE ATT&CK website: `https://attack.mitre.org/techniques/T1055/`.

- **Name some tools you use when analyzing malware.**

This is subjective based on the malware analyst answering, but some tools that can be used to analyze malware include the following:

  - Sysinternals: `https://docs.microsoft.com/en-us/sysinternals/`
  - PeStudio (Windows PE file static analysis tool): `https://www.winitor.com/`
  - Wireshark (Network traffic analyzer): `https://www.wireshark.org/`
  - IDA Pro (Disassembler): `https://www.hex-rays.com/products/ida/`
  - Flare VM: `https://github.com/mandiant/flare-vm`
  - REMnux: `https://remnux.org/`

- **Which header contains the field address of the EP?**

The `optional header` contains the address of the EP.

- **What does the hex value in the optional header tell you?**

This value identifies whether it is a 32-bit or 64-bit system.

- **Which field shows you the total size of the header in disk?**

The `SizeOfHeader` field that is located within the `optional header` field shows you this information.

- **Which field shows the number of sections in a PE file?**

The `NumberOfSections` field shows this information and there are up to 65,535 possible sections.

- **How can you tell if a file is an executable file or a** `.dll` **file?**

In the `Characteristics` field, the `IMAGE_FILE_EXECUTABLE_IMAGE` value will be set to 1 if it's an executable. If it's a .dll file, then the `IMAGE_FILE_DLL` field will have a value of 1.

You can learn more about image file headers from this Microsoft page: `https://docs.microsoft.com/en-us/windows/win32/api/winnt/ns-winnt-image_file_header`.

- **Describe the difference between the RVA and the absolute virtual address (AVA).**

The RVA is the relative address in relation to the `ImageBase` and the AVA is the original address in the virtual memory.

- **Calculate the RVA from the following information:**

ImageBase = 300,000

AVA = 300,300

The RVA is found by subtracting the ImageBase from the AVA. So, 300,300 minus 300,000 would leave you with 300 as the RVA.

- **What is the Import Address Table (IAT) used for?**

The IAT contains function pointers and it is used to get the addresses of different functions when DLLs are loaded.

- **What is the Import Names Table (INT) and how does it differ from IAT?**

The IAT points to the address of functions in memory and the INT points to the name of each function.

- **What are thread-local storage (TLS) callbacks?**

TLS callbacks have been around for years and are an anti-analysis technique that allows malicious code to be executed prior to the `AddressOfEntry` point in the sample.

- **What are virtual tables (Vtables) in the C++ language?**

  For the classes that contain virtual functions, the compiler will create a Vtable. These Vtables house the entry for each of the virtual functions accessible by a class and store a pointer to the definition of the virtual function. The entries found in the Vtable can point to functions that are declared in the class or point to functions that were inherited from a base class.

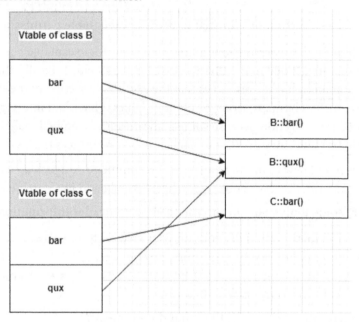

Figure 8.1 – Example of a Vtable

- **What information does the** .pdb **file contain?**

  Program database (.pdb) files contain the debugging information for the program in Microsoft Windows.

- **How do disassembler programs know the names of functions and variables when you load an image?**

  The IMAGE_DEBUG_DIRECTORY contains the addresses of the raw data points that point to the functions and variables.

- **What is the difference between the** VirtualSize **and the** SizeOfRawData **fields?**

  When the image is in disk, SizeOfRawData is the size of the section. When the section is loaded into memory, VirtualSize is the total size of that section in memory.

- **What is the purpose of the** `.reloc` **section?**

  The relocation (`.reloc`) section contains information (variables and instructions) about where files should be mapped to if they cannot be loaded using their preferred addresses that are defined with `ImageBase`.

  You can learn more about relocation sections at this Microsoft site: `https://docs.microsoft.com/en-us/windows/win32/debug/pe-format`.

- **Can the** `.rsrc` **section be adjusted to provide executable permissions?**

  Any section can have permissions adjusted to allow for executable permissions. Permissions are defined in the `Characteristics` field. Typically, the `.rsrc` section contains arbitrary resources that the executable section of the PE can reference, such as bitmaps, icons, or other graphics. I have had interviewers ask about the `.rsrc` section because some malware authors embed malicious binaries within this section since the PE executable section references the `.rsrc` section.

  If you are brand new to malware analysis, I recommend you pick up a copy of the *Practical Malware Analysis* book by Michael Sikorski and No Starch Press.

- **What are some tools that you can use to view PE header information?**

  The answer to this question depends on your favorite tools to use, but some are PE Tools (`https://petoolse.github.io/petools/`), FileAlyzer (`http://www.safer-networking.org/products/filealyzer/`), and PEView (`http://wjradburn.com/software/`).

- **When you locate 'MZ' in a PE file, what does it mean?**

  The **MZ** in the magic number area of the PE file stands for **Mark Zbikowski**, who was one of the lead developers of executables. The `MZ` header allowed for backward compatibility between Windows 32-bit and MS-DOS.

- **In assembly language, what is the difference between 'MOV' and 'LEA' instructions?**

  The **load effective address (LEA)** loads a pointer to the item you are addressing. **MOV** accesses memory and loads the real value of the item you are addressing. LEA is helpful for performing address calculations and storing the result for later use.

  You can learn more about the MOV and LEA instructions in the following resources:

  - `https://www.youtube.com/watch?v=eh3lnA_QykU`
  - `https://www.cs.uaf.edu/2016/fall/cs301/lecture/09_28_machinecode.html`

- `https://stackoverflow.com/questions/24746123/assembly-mov-instruction`
- `https://stackoverflow.com/questions/1658294/whats-the-purpose-of-the-lea-instruction`
- `https://www.youtube.com/watch?v=mKcWIA1vKOw`

- **Name some of the calling conventions in the assembly language.**

  Some of the calling conventions include `cdecl` (C declaration), `stdcall` (standard call), Microsoft `_fastcall`, and Microsoft `_thiscall`.

- **How are standard calls and a C declaration different?**

  In standard calls (`stdcall`), the arguments are pushed from right to left and the cleaning of the stack is done by the `callee` function. In a C declaration (`cdecl`), the arguments of a function are pushed from left to right and the cleaning of the stack is done by the `caller` function.

- **What is the typical default calling convention in Windows C++ programs?**

  Standard call (`stdcall`) is the default calling convention you typically find in a C++ program, but you can always change the default calling convention in your compiler or IDE.

- **What is the output of an XOR operation if the operands are different?**

  The output using different operands would be `1`.

- **Give an example of how to set the `eax` register value to zero.**

  `xor eax, eax` will add the content of `eax` to itself, which will set the value to `0`. This is more efficient than using `mov` to change the value, as in `mov eax, 0`, and helps to reduce false dependencies.

- **Can you tell me the difference between a structure and a union in C programming?**

  A union only allows you to set the value of one variable at a time from the pool of variables. If you try to set the value of another variable, it will replace the value of the first variable since there is a single memory space allocated for the union.

  A structure allows you to have multiple variables and you can set a value for each variable separately.

- **You have 4 GB of memory on a Windows system. How much is used for kernel space and how much is being used for user space?**

  1 GB is used for the kernel and 3 GB is used for user space.

- **If you identify a high level of entropy in your analysis of a section, what could this indicate?**

High entropy could indicate that the section is packed.

Cisco has a short blog post on entropy theory and how it can be used in malware analysis: `https://umbrella.cisco.com/blog/using-entropy-to-spot-the-malware-hiding-in-plain-sight`.

- **Can you tell me what the 'use-after-free' vulnerability is?**

Use-after-free vulnerabilities occur when freed memory is allocated to another pointer and the original pointer is then directed to newly allocated data. If this new data holds a class, then additional pointers may be spread within the heap data. If an attacker overwrites one of these pointers to point to their shellcode, then it is possible for the attacker to execute arbitrary code.

- **Can you name some common process injection techniques?**

Some of the common process injection techniques are DLL injection, PE injection, process hollowing, thread execution hijacking, hooking, registry modifications, **asynchronous procedure calls (APC)** injection, **Extra Window Memory Injection (EWMI)**, Shims injection, and inline hooking.

- **Can you tell me what process hollowing is?**

Process hollowing happens when it unmaps legitimate code from a process' memory and overwrites the space with malicious code.

This is a Black Hat conference presentation on process hollowing that can be helpful if you are not familiar with process hollowing: `https://youtu.be/9L9I1T5QDg4`.

- **What are some of the common Windows Registry locations that malware leverages for persistence?**

They are:

- `HKEY_CURRENT_USER\Software\Microsoft\Windows\CurrentVersion\Run`

- `HKEY_CURRENT_USER\Software\Microsoft/Windows\CurrentVersion\RunOnce`

You can read about some of the persistence techniques used by APT groups on the MITRE ATT&CK website: `https://attack.mitre.org/techniques/T1547/001/`.

- **How many types of breakpoints are available in a debugger?**

  There are four types of breakpoints in a debugger. These are the software breakpoint, hardware breakpoint, memory breakpoint, and conditional breakpoint.

- **How does malware disable the Task Manager in Windows?**

  Malware can modify the security settings of the operating system by altering security policies stored in `HKEY_CURRENT_USER\Software\Microsoft\Windows\CurrentVersion\Policies\System`.

- **What are some indicators in a PE header that might reveal a sample is malicious?**

  If an executable is packed, you might see uncommon sections such as `.upx`, the `.rsrc` section might have processes without icons but with scripts or databases embedded within them, the `imports` of the section could be obstructed or missing, and the sections could have high entropy that could indicate malware.

There are many intricacies of malware analysis that could be asked during your interview. From experience in interviews, it's important for you as a malware analyst to be able to explain your process for analyzing a malware sample, including dynamic and static analysis, and be prepared to answer questions around PEs.

Summary

In this chapter, you learned about the malware analyst career and the average salary range in the United States. You also learned how this can be a stepping stone into more advanced careers and learned some of the technical skills needed for the job.

In the next chapter, you will learn about a career as a cybersecurity manager, including common knowledge-based interview questions you might be asked.

Part 3: Cybersecurity Management Careers and Interview Questions

This part will cover the cybersecurity manager, cybersecurity sales engineer, and CISO roles and common interview questions for these careers. This part will also cover the most common behavioral interview questions asked during interviews and provide some final words of wisdom from the authors for your cybersecurity career.

This part of the book comprises the following chapters:

- *Chapter 9, Cybersecurity Manager*
- *Chapter 10, Cybersecurity Sales Engineer*
- *Chapter 11, CISO*
- *Chapter 12, Behavioral Interview Questions*
- *Chapter 13, Final Thoughts*

9
Cybersecurity Manager

This chapter focuses on cybersecurity management roles. This type of role is a mid-to-senior-level role, typically requiring years of experience both in the subject matter as well as leadership.

The following topics will be covered in this chapter:

- What is a cybersecurity manager?
- How much can you make in this career?
- What other careers can this type of role lead to?
- Certification considerations
- Example roles
- Common interview questions for a cybersecurity manager

What is a cybersecurity manager?

The role of a cybersecurity manager spans a broad range of types and responsibilities. At a high level, cybersecurity managers will either lead an entire cybersecurity program or a specific functional group that is part of a broader program strategy. Specifically, an organization might put a leader in place to lead their security operations program, which would include developing a strategy aligned with the desired security outcomes of the business from a tactical perspective. We will refer to this type of leader as a **cybersecurity program manager**.

Within the overall security operations program strategy, there will be specific functional groups responsible for the day-to-day operations and execution of the strategy, such as threat intelligence teams, security analysts, and security engineers. These functional groups also require managers, and we'll refer to these managers as **cybersecurity team managers** to avoid confusion.

Cybersecurity program manager

A **cybersecurity program manager** is an individual that effectively leads, communicates, and is responsible for an organization's cybersecurity programs. As part of a cybersecurity program's management, they are responsible for helping with the development of cybersecurity projects and infrastructure, as well as ensuring alignment with business programs and strategies. No matter how secure an organization may be, if the strategy introduces friction or roadblocks to daily operations and productivity, user adoption and executive buy-in will likely be an uphill battle.

The cybersecurity program manager is usually heavily involved with the CISO and other members of leadership to ensure that programs are in line with their vision of how security should be handled. Some of the components of a cybersecurity program are compliance, governance, security operations, asset security, and infrastructure security. These individuals are usually not involved at the operational level with all aspects of the program but more so at the strategic level, ensuring the program is running smoothly and on target.

Some of the certifications that can come in handy for an individual in this role are the following:

- **Project Management Professional (PMP)**: https://www.pmi.org/certifications/project-management-pmp
- **Certified Information Systems Security Professional (CISSP)**: https://www.isc2.org/Certifications/CISSP

- **Certified Information Security Manager (CISM)**: `https://www.isaca.org/credentialing/certifications`

- **Certified Information Systems Auditor (CISA)**: `https://www.isaca.org/credentialing/cisa`

- **CompTIA Security+: SANS** (`https://www.sans.org/cyber-security-certifications/?msc=main-nav`) and **GIAC** (`https://www.giac.org/certifications/`) certifications

The types of cybersecurity programs may include, but are certainly not limited to, the following:

- Security awareness and user training

- Incident response

- Security governance and risk management

- Identity and access management

- Security operations and security engineering

- Software development security

Cybersecurity team manager

A **cybersecurity team manager** is an individual responsible for a specific team within an organization's security program and any individuals that might be reporting to them. The size or maturity of the organization usually determines the team that a cybersecurity manager might be responsible for, and/or whether they would have responsibilities at the individual contributor level while being considered a process manager.

There are several types of cybersecurity team managers; the first depends on whether the manager is a **technical manager** or a **people manager**. Depending on the size or maturity of the company and the type of product that they are delivering/creating, companies look for technical managers who have a deep understanding of technical requirements. These technical managers often grow directly from other technical roles into this type of leadership role, becoming responsible for managing different subspecialties.

The other type of manager in this category is the people manager who has a fundamental understanding of all the technical areas but does not go as deep as the cybersecurity specialists or consultants they might be managing. On the other hand, these managers can handle the required business relations, people, and processes. They can help teams remove some of the blocks and organizational processes that would otherwise slow or stop them from delivering results.

Cybersecurity manager roles and responsibilities vary, depending on the needs of the organization. As seen in the following descriptions, some organizations may choose to align managers to specialized areas of cybersecurity, such as critical infrastructure, applications, or the cloud:

- **Critical infrastructure security manager**: Cybersecurity managers in this type of role are mostly responsible for ensuring the availability of the infrastructure by performing several due diligence activities, such as assessing and mitigating risk, monitoring for potential threats, and creating and testing incident response plans.

- **Network security manager**: Network security managers are typically focused on edge infrastructure and end user activity (firewall, IDS/IPS, web/content filtering, and so on) and are responsible for protecting corporate assets from external cyberattacks and insider threats. It is important that network security managers strike a balance between security and functionality, meaning that mitigating controls selected for implementation should not negatively impact employee productivity.

- **Application security manager**: Application security managers are tasked with leading teams of software developers to ensure secure coding teams by following best practices, such as dynamic and static analysis, input validation and output sanitation, proper encryption and authentication requirements, and access control.

- **Cloud security manager**: Migrating data to the public cloud introduces different data protection challenges compared to on-premises environments. One of the most common risks is data exposure resulting from a poorly defined cloud security strategy or misconfigured cloud security controls. Cloud security managers monitor cloud environments for vulnerabilities, threats, risks, and proper data access and cloud workload configuration controls.

On the other hand, cybersecurity managers could potentially be aligned to the functional areas of the cybersecurity program, such as security operations, the red team, and the blue team. The following list provides examples of cybersecurity manager roles:

- **Security Operations Center (SOC) manager**: The security operations team is a critical component of a cybersecurity program. At a high level, the team is responsible for the detection of and response to threats within the corporate environment, regardless of where they are discovered within the infrastructure.

  An SOC manager is responsible for managing SOC analysts, in addition to defining policies, creating and refining security operations team processes, and working with security engineers to continue to grow the organization's capabilities.

- **Blue team/red team manager**: The blue team defends the enterprise. This team is responsible for monitoring and maintaining the company's security and network defense system against cyberthreats, typically by working with (defending against) the company's red team.

  The red team sits on the offensive side of the cybersecurity coin. This team helps the blue team by simulating cyberattacks designed to test the effectiveness of the security controls in place.

Individuals on these teams report to their team managers, who are responsible for working together to define the scope and rules of engagement for testing the organization's defenses.

Job titles and teams

There are several different job titles managers may hold according to the `https://www.cyberseek.org/pathway.html` website:

- Security manager
- Information systems security officer
- Information security manager
- Security administrator
- Information security officer

The types of cybersecurity teams may include, but are not limited to, the following:

- Threat intelligence
- Network security architecture
- Digital forensics
- Blue team analysts
- Red team analysts

The following mind map may be helpful in understanding the different cybersecurity domains: `https://www.linkedin.com/pulse/cybersecurity-domain-map-ver-30-henry-jiang`.

The considerations for certifications for cybersecurity team manager roles are very similar to those for cybersecurity program managers:

- CISSP
- CISM and CISA
- CompTIA Security+
- SANS/GIAC certifications
- Other management-focused certifications

As usual, when recommending certifications, I suggest evaluating the information and knowledge gained and the value they will add to your career. Some of the values include bypassing HR filters to demonstrate to hiring managers that you have a level of knowledge in the field, or even just personal bragging rights while learning new information.

How much can you make in this career?

Cybersecurity program managers can earn $90,000 to $150,000 on average based on their experience, location, and a number of other factors. It could definitely be higher, considering that companies who might need program managers at this level include other bonuses and financial rewards in their compensation packages.

The salary range for cybersecurity team managers is extensive, as it runs from that of an individual contributor system or process owner, starting at $60,000, right up to the top end of the spectrum at $170,000 for those managing programs and who have one or more teams of stakeholders reporting to them. The location, specialization, experience, and area of responsibility will affect the salary earned in any specific position.

What other careers can you do?

With career growth, some of the positions cybersecurity managers can look forward to will only begin with additional responsibilities if they are individual contributors and only responsible for the security of one system. After managing multiple systems, managers can then begin leading teams. Continued growth usually leads to a manager becoming a director, who, in addition to being responsible for multiple managers and their direct reports, will also be responsible for additional tasks, such as budgeting for the programming, road-mapping for the growth of the program, as well as interfacing and managing the relationships of the different leaders in the business.

Common interview questions

Here are some common questions that you may face during an interview for the position of cybersecurity manager:

- **What are the different types of programs you have previously been responsible for?**

  Rather than simply describing the technologies and systems you have been responsible for, talk about the business problems, how specific technology was implemented to solve them, and the results achieved. For those responsible for multiple systems, discuss how the different systems were used/integrated/connected to help solve a more significant business problem and achieve results. If you are inheriting a legacy environment, discuss how you potentially optimized its use, maintained or replaced the system, and your results.

  For those responsible for managing teams who then work with the systems, discuss the strategy you used to manage the team and systems, manage the business relationships, and help achieve the business mission.

- **How do you help to drive cultural changes in your security programs?**

  Cultural change starts with C-suite and management buy-in to start integrating security and risk-based decisions into how they run the business. It all starts with awareness of the potential impact of security issues. Risk-based choices for a company could be the following:

  - Risk-informed-acceptance of a risk by the business

  - Risk avoidance by avoiding risky business areas

  - Risk mitigation by actively taking steps to reduce the risk

  - Risk transference by outsourcing aspects of a risk or using insurance

  - Risk ignorance by not acknowledging potential risks in an environment

  - For more information on the risk management process, see the following: `https://www.pmi.org/learning/library/practical-risk-management-approach-8248`.

  Through security awareness both at the management level and by encouraging awareness at the individual level, risks can be effectively managed. Having awareness at the individual level makes it personally applicable to an individual, rather than just part of their work role. Making the content or awareness training engaging rather than just informational will encourage more people in the organization to adopt a cultural change.

- **How would you demonstrate root cause analysis?**

Cybersecurity managers hope to work with a team that is responsible for supporting the *incident response* to a situation, especially with a security implication, while the technology in question might not always be something that they are managing directly. Some organizations conduct *postmortems* to better understand what happened during an event, what went right, what went wrong, what was the root cause (without assigning blame), and how things could be improved to avoid similar issues occurring.

"Basic problem solving. Demonstrate a methodical way of going from a symptom to root cause and correction... It allows you to gauge [the] feedback mechanism (whether a system or stakeholders or both) to validate [the] plan of action."

– Omkhar Arasaratnam

- **What would you do in order to ensure that your organization was prepared for an evaluation against a standard such as SOC 2 compliance?**

With any standard, process, or assessment, it is helpful to understand the standards against which compliance or success will be measured, and then to look inside your organization to see how close the standards are to being met. Using this gap assessment will guide the rest of the implementation.

Service Organization Control 2 (SOC 2) is a set of compliance requirements and auditing processes targeted at third-party service providers that helps companies understand external risks. You are now the third-party vendor for another company, and they are looking at this report to help analyze the risk they will be assuming by partnering with your organization. It helps companies determine whether their business partners and vendors can securely manage data and protect the interests and privacy of their clients.

SOC 2 was developed by the **American Institute of Certified Public Accountants (AICPA)** (`https://www.aicpa.org/`). Within its processes, there are two types of SOC 2 reports:

- **SOC 2 Type 1** details the systems and controls you should have in place for security compliance. In order to prepare for this audit, you will need to provide auditors with evidence of these systems and controls and allow them to verify whether you meet the relevant *trust principles*. Think of this as a point-in-time verification of controls.

- However, as a good cybersecurity manager, you should strive to ensure that these controls continue to be maintained or grow in maturity over time. This will prepare you for the next type of assessment.

- **SOC 2 Type 2** – in this assessment, the auditor assesses how effective your program's processes are at providing the desired level of data security and management over a period of time.

By planning to have validation of your controls continuously monitored, you will be able to ensure that your controls function as designed. Additionally, you use the monitoring data to make improvements, you can then add additional automated reporting to encourage the growth and implementation of the controls.

Security compliance programs such as SOC2 should just be a baseline for an organization.

The major focus of the SOC2 compliance certification standard is listed as follows. In order to be successful, you should be able to demonstrate to the auditor that you meet the criteria that the AICPA has set:

- **Security**: The organization's system must have controls in place to safeguard against unauthorized physical and logical access. Be careful not to overlook controls for physical access and to understand the shared responsibility model when using cloud services.

- **Availability**: The system must be available for operation and must be used as agreed. Whether you're using cloud services or your own systems, be sure to test failover capabilities and ensure that they function as intended.

- **Processing integrity**: System processing must be complete, accurate, well-timed, and authorized.

- **Confidentiality**: Information held by the organization that is classified as *confidential* by a user must be protected. Having a proper data definition and classification procedure from the beginning is extremely helpful compared to implementing one after a protection mechanism has already been deployed.

- **Privacy**: All personal information that the organization collects, uses, retains, and discloses must be in accordance with its privacy notice and principles. These are specified by the AICPA and the **Canadian Institute of Chartered Accountants (CICA)**. As global privacy standards expand, be sure to consider the implications they will have for your business models. For example, while you might not be doing business in Europe, you may still be subject to the General Data Protection Regulation.

The SOC2 is just one of many compliance standards that you might look to apply in your organization. The key is just to use them as a baseline for your security program, not a high watermark.

- **How do I develop a cybersecurity strategy for my program?**

  The development of a cybersecurity strategy is, at its heart, an alignment with the business strategy. The first step is talking to business leaders and seeing where the business is heading or where it needs improvement, and then developing a strategy from that. For example, if your salespeople are informing you that SOC2 is preventing them from working with larger clients, a solution for that could be included in the strategy. If your developers are looking to start bringing development in-house, you could help them with integrating security checkpoints during the SDLC process to find and discover bugs or coding issues before they become vulnerabilities.

  Based on the desired future state of the business, you can conduct a GAP assessment that will help you look at the work needed to complete objectives. Ensure that you check with each of the lines of business for as much alignment as possible. It may even be possible to get them to pay for your security strategy if it helps with achieving their objectives. Once alignment is achieved, ensure that a buffer in the budget is included for dealing with unexpected incidents. In the event of budget cuts, ensure that you make management aware of functionalities or advances they will be sacrificing. To cover yourself, get decisions regarding budget cuts confirmed in writing/email in case they lead to a problem in the future.

- **How do cybersecurity program managers ensure alignment with business priorities?**

  As program manager, you are responsible for ensuring that projects deployed within a cybersecurity program meet an organization's business needs as a whole. This organizational overview starts with clarifying the intent of the cybersecurity project and understanding the business problems they are looking to solve. The program manager must act as a business partner and influencer, delivering on their programs. They need to know what is happening within different lines of the business and the potential impact changes can have on the program.

  While it is helpful for this individual to be more technically minded so that they can look at the changing technological landscape, future technologies, and how they can help to optimize their portfolio, it is not always necessary. Lack of technical understanding can be supplemented with the support of a team and/or outside consultants. Program management needs to be forward-thinking in helping businesses achieve their goals and have its finger on the pulse of current technology.

One of the early stages of this includes working with different lines of the business, understanding the impact of these changes (positive/negative), and then providing a top-level assessment before a project sponsor signs off on a project. At the more significant organization level, changes to applications or services provided by the security department can have a knock-on effect on the workflow in different lines of the business, and this needs to be thoroughly understood and made a part of any risk-based decision before a project is approved or implemented. Starting with pilot programs can be a great way to test the effects of such changes within an organization and limit the results to a small subset.

- **How do cybersecurity program managers work to ensure that they can enable business programs?**

The most critical aspect of a cybersecurity program manager's role is understanding a business application portfolio and ensuring that they can enable an optimized business mission by implementing security controls and procedures appropriately. This means thinking ahead and remaining aligned with future business strategies and initiatives, ensuring the company's level of cyber-resilience improves (or, at a minimum, gets maintained) as it continues to evolve.

For example, suppose your company is primarily on-premises in aging data centers and looking into ways of using **cloud service providers** (**CSPs**) to help it migrate to a more scalable and resilient operating model. In that case, the cybersecurity program should be helping in that journey to enable secure options as the company shifts its business model. Whether it is considering **Platform as a Service** (**PaaS**), **Infrastructure as a Service** (**IaaS**), or **Software as a Service** (**SaaS**), work with them to understand the shared responsibility models from each of the cloud providers so that they know their areas of responsibilities versus the CSP and where potential risks lie.

This responsibility includes understanding and working with the CISO and other security leaders on what changes they need to implement to optimize the business or update their security tools to meet changing needs.

- **How do you set up an application security program?**

When working with developers or setting up an application security-focused security program, the concept of *shifting as far left as possible* is usually the first thing that comes to mind. When you are thinking about it from a people-process-technology perspective, starting with people is the first step you'll want to consider.

Let's say, for example, that developers are working with you to start addressing things such as preferred coding languages, their thoughts on security, providing developer-focused security training, and so on. Supposing you have the data or statistics on the most common vulnerabilities discovered in their code in the past year, you can use them as examples with a member of the red team, showing how those vulnerabilities are exploitable. If you didn't have that data, you could start with the **OWSAP top 10 vulnerabilities** (`https://owasp.org/Top10/`). Providing developers with context and training on how to reduce those vulnerabilities and become security experts themselves expands the reach of the security department.

Combining processes and tools helps to complete a cycle by providing the right tools at the right time. Let's start with the **Integrated Development Environment (IDE)**; by providing tools that can help identify potential errors and vulnerabilities during coding and secure code training, you reduce the need for it to be reworked later as a bug or vulnerability. Next, having quick **Static App Scanning (SAS)** at the unit level ensures that code doesn't have glaring vulnerabilities. As the code comes together, having **Dynamic App Scanning (DAS)**, **Runtime Application Self Protection (RASP)**, mobile code scanning, and scanning containers, images, software repositories, and libraries helps make it more holistic.

It is beneficial to have a working group of development and security leaders deciding on the standards and implications, and changing the management approach to tackle applications that might have vulnerabilities and whether they have the approval to be deployed into an environment. There will be times when a business will need to deploy an application with known exposures to meet business needs. This working group can help with compensating controls for the environment and a business-as-usual remediation plan for any necessary software improvements.

- **How do you measure success in your security program?**

Measurement of the success of a security program should be based on the people, process, and technology involved in the business. Starting at the people level with organizational culture, which usually consists of the security awareness program. At the process level, the focus should be on business enablement while at the technology level, it should be how security aids in securing the various levels of the organization's technology footprint.

While each company will have different metrics depending on its size, maturity, and industry, ultimately they should focus on how the security program has helped to mitigate or minimize risks for their company.

Helping the company's stakeholders implement security practices in their daily lives, whether that be at home or work, will help drive safe behaviors with technology. For example, providing users with password managers for personal use will make them feel more comfortable and minimize the harmful habit of password reuse. Many password managers include **Two-Factor Authentication (2FA)** features that allow them to display a rotating second-factor authentication token, helping to add a layer of security compared to simply using a username and password. Other aspects of assisting the people layer of an organization relate to helping them identify potential phishing emails and scams. Phishing and cons are increasingly arriving via social media and SMS, so helping employees be safe in their personal lives will also improve their behavior at work.

As mentioned previously, implementing secure password use and multi-factor authentication processes encourages the use of safe methods and mitigates risks around user identity takeovers and password reuse. Technology is also implemented as part of that process to help secure user identities. Some measurements you can look for are a reduction in account takeovers, a reduction in clicks on phishing emails, and an increase in the reporting of phishing emails.

This people-and-process approach should be used as a model for all other aspects of the business, and measuring success should minimize unsafe practices.

Improvements in vulnerability management programs should be made following a similar approach – understanding what can help improve processes and providing people with the necessary training and resources to improve outcomes. Measuring the ability of your team to mitigate known vulnerabilities within or before their assigned SLAs will demonstrate your program's ability to manage and reduce risks in this area.

- **How do you manage vulnerability management programs and the risk management involved?**

   At the program level, one of the many challenges an organization faces is ensuring that it has an excellent vulnerability management program, followed by program execution that leads to effectively managing the identified risks. There are a couple of foundational elements of vulnerability management program management that we need to cover before discussing how we would manage the risk surrounding it for the organization.

The foundation of any vulnerability management starts with an asset management program. The first two controls on the CIS Top 18 controls (https://www.cisecurity.org/controls/cis-controls-list) demonstrate how important they are to an organization as they are at the top of the list. A good vulnerability management program needs a solid asset inventory management program that includes software, hardware, and understanding the implications of third-party software (having a software bill of materials helps to understand this: https://www.ntia.gov/SBOM) and services. This asset management program will allow you to understand all of the hardware, software, code, and other things that are within an organization's boundaries. Managers need to understand the current software or firmware levels of all these assets, what patches are available for the assets, and the potential vulnerabilities within that remain unpatched.

Sometimes, patches can break functionality or interoperability between assets. As software and hardware vendors release patches or updates to their software or hardware, it is crucial to understand the vulnerability that the patch or update is looking to mitigate and whether it might break any functionality or interoperability between other assets in an environment. It is recommended that a patch be tested in a restricted sandbox environment to ensure that it works before rolling it out to the network.

Other aspects of vulnerability management that need to be considered are the prioritization of the application of the patches and the associated downtime, followed closely by understanding the resources from the different aspects of the business that would be responsible for the application process. Often, the resources responsible for the application of the patches are not under the responsibility of the vulnerability management program. The program needs to develop an organizationally accepted **service-level agreement (SLA)** and work with resources to ensure that the patches are applied within the appropriate time frame.

Organizations need to develop a criticality rating (for example, critical, high, medium, and low) for risks and when those patches need to remediate. This SLA is often created based on the criticality of the vulnerability for which the patch's risk is meant to remediate. Some companies have developed a 7, 30, 60, and 90-day approach for applying the appropriate patches. Unfortunately, that does not consider the compensating controls within the organizational environment, so while a vulnerability might be rated as critical externally without controls, it might be different inside the environment.

As a potential cybersecurity manager, during your interview, it becomes critical that you pull back from the interviewer's line of questioning and discuss these points:

- Where are the pain points of the security program and the business?

- What have they done to address them, and what have they tried that's failed?

- How can you help them solve their issues?

Summary

In this chapter, you learned what a cybersecurity manager is, their average salaries in the United States, certifications to consider, career path options, role types, and common questions you might be asked during an interview. Be sure to understand the difference between roles that require more people leadership than technical leadership and vice versa, as well as whether the role is more specialized or functional in nature.

In the next chapter, we will turn our attention to a role that is one of the industry's best-kept secrets – cybersecurity sales engineer.

10
Cybersecurity Sales Engineer

This chapter focuses on the role of the cybersecurity sales engineer. The role is also commonly referred to as sales or solution consultant, solution architect, or simply presales. Although some organizations are moving away from using *engineer* in the title in favor of more business-focused titles, the sales engineer title is still very common and is therefore the title that will be used throughout the remainder of the chapter. When searching for jobs of this type, it would be wise to search all versions of the title to ensure the most complete search results.

The following topics will be covered in this chapter:

- What is a cybersecurity sales engineer?
- How much can you make in this career?
- What education and/or certifications should be considered?
- Common interview questions

What is a cybersecurity sales engineer?

The cybersecurity sales engineer is a technical sales resource that sells cybersecurity technologies and/or services to businesses. This role is a hidden gem in the cybersecurity and broader tech industry; many technical resources shy away from this type of role mostly due to misconceptions regarding sales requirements. In most organizations, sales engineers are considered sales overlays, basically meaning they support the sales process, but do not own it. This means that although sales engineers are often tied to the quota of the sales reps they support, they are not directly responsible for activities such as prospecting or cold calling, pipeline generation, and forecasting.

Sales engineers typically support one or more account managers (or sales representatives). While the account manager is responsible for managing the specifics of the sale (pricing negotiations, contract negotiations, term length, contract signature, and so on), the sales engineer is responsible for understanding the requirements of the business they are selling to and demonstrating how their products or services meet those requirements. These activities can include, but are certainly not limited to, providing a demo, delivering a **Proof of Value (PoV)** or **Proof of Concept (PoC)**, documenting the scope of the project and implementation requirements, and articulating how their company's product or service is better than its competitors'. Sales engineers have significant influence over a buyer's decision to select their product or service and are therefore a critical function of the broader sales team.

How much can you make in this career?

Before diving into specific dollar amounts, it is important to understand the pay structure for a cybersecurity sales engineer. It is not the pay structure most technical resources are used to, which in my experience is either a base salary or, in some cases, a base salary and a performance-based annual bonus. According to a recent industry study, the most common compensation structure for sales engineers in general is base salary plus a variable component; the split is usually somewhere in the ballpark of 80/20 or 70/30, with base salary being more heavily weighted. Base salary is a straightforward fixed amount, but the variable component will differ from company to company.

The variable component of the total compensation package is performance-driven. For sales representatives, the variable pay is usually commission-based, meaning they are paid based on how much they sell. The same is also true for sales engineers in many cases, but the variable pay is sometimes tied to **management by objectives (MBOs)**. In this model, variable pay is based on the achievement of tasks assigned to the sales engineer in alignment with company goals. In rare instances, variable pay can be a combination of commission and MBOs.

A few other helpful terms to be aware of are listed here:

- **Quota** – The sales goal or target a seller must achieve over a specified period (for example, quarterly or annually)
- **On-Target Commission (OTC)** – The amount of commission a seller can expect to earn if they reach their sales target
- **On-Target Earnings (OTE)** – The sum of base salary plus OTC

Let's walk through an example. A seller receives a compensation plan detailing the following: annual quota = $3,000,000, OTC = $100,000. This means if the seller achieves $3,000,000 in sales, they can expect to earn $100,000 in commission for the year. To take it a step further, if the seller's base salary is $100,000, their OTE is $200,000. Compensation plans can become incredibly complex when you get into details around things like accelerators (which allow for overperformance) and overachievement bonuses, but we won't get into those.

It's important to note that technical sales is a high-risk, high-reward career when compared to traditional security roles. Referring to the previous example, $200,000 OTE may seem like an attractive offer, but keep in mind that $100,000 of that total is not guaranteed. If for some reason the seller is unable to close a single deal, they will only earn their base salary of $100,000. The upside, however, is that the seller could achieve more than $3,000,000 in sales, which would (at least, should) result in more than $100,000 in commission.

At the time of writing, the average base salary for an experienced sales engineer is $140,000. The average for an experienced cybersecurity sales engineer is a bit higher, with the average in the $150,000–$160,000 range. From a total earnings perspective, if we take the $160,000 base salary and assume an 80/20 split, the OTC would be $40,000, yielding OTE of $200,000.

What education and/or certifications should be considered?

The path to becoming a cybersecurity sales engineer is not a linear one. Some individuals transition into the role from hands-on technical roles, while others come from business or educational backgrounds and learn the technical skills on the job. In general, a successful sales engineer will have a solid understanding of advanced security and/or security technology concepts and specialize in a specific product or service. They are technically minded, but also business savvy, and possess a balance of both the technical and soft skills necessary to build relationships, solve business problems with technology solutions, and simplify complex technical concepts. Sales experience is a definite advantage, in addition to experience in a customer-facing role.

There are several organizations and individuals working to bring more visibility to technical sales as a career. Within the technical sales community, a very small percentage of sales engineers are cybersecurity specialists, so there is no shortage of opportunities available to the right candidates. The following list highlights some resources worth exploring if a career in technical sales is of interest:

- **PreSales Collective** (`presalescollective.com`) – PreSales Collective is a global community of PreSales (technical sales) professionals that connect with one another to learn, grow, and move the profession forward. The organization provides access to webinars, blogs, podcasts, eBooks, and other resources aimed at helping members grow their careers as presales professionals. The *PreSales Academy* by PreSales Collective is an 8-week program that prepares individuals for a career in technical sales.

- *The 6 Habits of Highly Effective Sales Engineers* by *Chris White* is a book that helps sales engineers improve their sales skills. It is a great read for anyone interested in entering the field.

Given the consultative nature of the role, degrees and certifications in the sales engineer's area of expertise help establish credibility with buyers. Specific to cybersecurity, the following are certifications you could expect a senior sales engineer to possess (this is by no means intended to be an exhaustive list):

- **Certified Information Systems Security Professional (CISSP)** (`https://www.isc2.org/Certifications/CISSP`)

- **Certified Information Security Manager (CISM)** (`https://www.isaca.org/credentialing/cism`)

- **Certified Cloud Security Professional (CCSP)** (`https://www.isc2.org/Certifications/CcSP`)

- **GIAC Security Leadership Certification (GSLC)** (`https://www.giac.org/certifications/security-leadership-gslc/`)

- **Security+** (`https://www.comptia.org/certifications/security`) and **Systems Security Certified Practitioner (SSCP)** (`https://www.isc2.org/Certifications/sscp`) are also relevant for newcomers to cybersecurity who may not meet the experience requirements of some of the more advanced certifications listed previously. Often, training and certification specific to the product or service being sold will be required as part of the on-the-job training.

Common interview questions

The sales engineer interview experience can sometimes be long and demanding, but finding the right fit makes it all worthwhile in the end. The number of interviews can range from three to more than five. I once went through eight interviews, which included a presentation to a team of sales engineers, before receiving an offer. Eight interviews might sound like a lot, but it's important that sales engineers integrate seamlessly into the teams they'll be working with and supporting. In a role where relationships can make or break a sale, cultural fit is as important as technical fit.

Throughout the process, you should expect to speak to any combination of sales reps and sales leaders, sales engineers and sales engineering leaders, a member of the human resources team, and maybe even members of the company's customer success and product organizations. Some interviews will be one on one, and others will be with a panel. The ultimate key to crushing the interview and landing this type of role is to be confident, relatable, charismatic, and memorable. Remember – people buy from people.

As previously mentioned, cybersecurity sales engineers require a mix of technical, interpersonal (or soft), and sales skills; you should expect questions that challenge your capabilities in each of these areas. Communication and presentation skills are at the top of the priority list in terms of skills a presales leader will want to validate, so you can expect some sort of presentation or pitch to be part of the interview process (a great storyteller always stands out when delivering a presentation). Depending on the company's product or service offering, technical requirements may be technology-focused (such as endpoint protection, firewalls, and so on) or outcome-focused (such as threat hunting or risk management services). In some cases, the role will require both.

I cannot stress to you enough the importance of what I'm about to tell you. Although this is a technical sales role, it is still a sales role. Your job will be to convince prospective buyers that your solution is best positioned to address their business needs, which means you will need to be convincing and believable. You must be a great listener, inspire confidence, and speak in the language and at the level of those you're speaking to. These tips are important to keep in mind during the interview process because the way you answer questions and articulate your value should be tailored to the interests of the interviewer. For example, you would want your technical skills to shine in an interview with a potential peer, but you may want your personality and sales or negotiating skills to shine instead in an interview with a sales rep or sales leader.

Selling is an emotional and psychological process. When you listen to a question, listen to absorb, listen to process. Don't make the dreaded mistake of simply listening to answer. Make sure you understand why the question is being asked so you not only can determine what to say but how to say it as well. Lastly, if you don't know the answer to a question, here are a few ways you can handle the situation:

- Request that the question be repeated. This gives you additional time to think and come up with your next move. – *"Would you mind repeating the question for me? I want to make sure I fully understand."*

- Repeat the question. This also gives you additional time to process. – *"Let me make sure I have this right. I want to ensure I'm answering the question the right way. Is what you're asking <insert your interpretation of the question>? And are you asking this because you're concerned about <insert your interpretation of the concern> or should I be thinking about this a different way?"*

- Throw a question back at them. This is one of my favorite tactics, especially when dealing with a difficult personality. Believe it or not, sometimes a meeting attendee's sole purpose is to trip you up or invalidate your offering. I've had this happen to me in an interview. I handled it like a champ, of course, but it caught me a little off guard, initially. Watch out for these types, and don't be afraid to challenge their way of thinking.

  In some instances, I've even had questions be withdrawn after asking for clarification or additional context. I'll warn you, though, this approach could backfire, so be careful. At the end of the day, you want to win over everyone you're engaged with, so you don't want anyone to feel like you're being combative. In some cases, there's a bit of an art and finesse required to pull this one off. – *"That's a great question. I'd be happy to walk you through that. But before I do, would you mind telling me if you're handling that situation in your environment today? It would be helpful for me to have that context as well as I demonstrate my approach."*

- Simply say *"I don't know."* A common pitfall for sales engineers is believing they need to have all the answers. It's great to have most of the answers, for sure, but admitting you don't know something can boost your credibility and help establish trust. There's an art to this as well, of course, you never want to literally say *"I don't know". – "Hmmm... I don't think anyone's ever asked me that question before. I'll have to look into that and get back to you. Looks like we'll both be learning something new today!"*

The following is a list of interview questions that will help you prepare for a cybersecurity sales engineer interview categorized by the following types.

General/behavioral questions

Questions in this category generally assess the type of person you are, what your motivations are – basically, how are you wired? Cultural fit and personality are the primary focus here, but that doesn't mean you shouldn't take advantage of opportunities to put your other shining qualities on display as well:

- **Why are you interested in working with us?**

  I love this question. Why? Because it's the perfect opportunity to showcase so many things at once. In a very simple and concise way, you can describe a little about yourself, show that you've done your homework and researched the company, toss in a bit of flattery by describing what about the company sparked your interest, and put your sales and business skills on display by selling the interviewer's company right back to them. The hidden advantage is this question typically comes up pretty early in the conversation, so your answer could potentially set the tone for the remainder of the call.

  Example: *"When I researched ABC Company, I was intrigued by the unique approach to mobile device management. The market is pretty saturated with vendors having similar offerings, but I see ABC's solution as a disruptive technology the industry has needed for a long time. This aligns well with my personality and motivations as someone that enjoys leveraging technology to solve complex business problems. I see a tremendous amount of opportunity to do exactly that with ABC."*

- **Why are you considering leaving your current role?**

  Be careful with this question. You'd be surprised at the number of candidates I've spoken with that have no problems bashing the current or previous employer. Maybe your boss drives you nuts, or perhaps you're bored or feel you're underpaid. All valid reasons for wanting to move on, but what value does that bring to a conversation during an interview? Not much.

Remember, the interviewer is asking questions to learn about you, not your previous employers. So, every chance you get, tell them more about you. And it wouldn't hurt to say something positive about your current role, either.

Example: *"I really am happy in my current role, and to be honest, I wasn't actively looking. But when the recruiter approached me about this role, I felt like I'd be doing myself a disservice if I didn't at least have the conversation, especially after researching the company a bit more. If I leave my current company, it will need to be for the right opportunity, and I feel like this could be it."*

- **What do you do for fun?**

  This is a simple question but can be challenging to answer if you're not prepared for it. When asking this question, the interviewer wants to know who you are outside the office. What are you passionate about? What are your hobbies? Are there any fun facts you can share? Family and pets tend to be pretty good conversation starters if you get stuck. Ultimately, you want to be relatable. And if you've done your homework on the interviewer, this is a great opportunity to touch on any shared interests you've uncovered.

- **What questions do you have for me?**

  When I conduct an interview, I learn most about a person based on the questions they ask – how they process information, what their priorities are, and, often, whether they're truly interested in the opportunity. Prepare your questions in advance and work with your recruiter or whoever your internal contact is to get a sense of whom you'll be talking to upfront; this way you can plan strategically to align your questions to the individuals you'll be speaking with. Ask questions that demonstrate your understanding of the business and your desire to be a valuable contributor to the organization.

  Long interview processes can make this challenging. As a senior executive, I'm often one of the last people candidates speak with and a lot of times they've emptied the tank by the time they get to me. If you find yourself out of questions about the company, ask questions about the person. Ask them what they enjoy about working at the company, or some of the challenges they face. What motivates them to come to work every day?

  Lastly, don't forget the soft close. Ask the interviewer flat out if they have any concerns about your ability to fulfill the duties of the role. If the answer is no, good for you. But if the answer is yes, you can address the concerns on the spot. After you've nailed that part, ask about next steps. It shows you're interested and gives you a sense of what's coming, timing, and so on, so you can prepare.

- **How do you handle a situation where a buyer isn't responding to your messaging the way you thought they would?**

  There are lots of hidden questions under the surface of this question. First off, you want to tell a story. If too many of your answers are theoretical instead of based on a true story, you may come off as inexperienced. For example, don't say *"I would probably..."*, or *"I think I would..."*. Provide a real-world example of a situation you handled. Talk about how it started out, how you recognized there was a disconnect, and what you did to get things back on track. You want to tell a story that ends with a win – even if it's more of a moral victory.

- **Who is the best manager you've worked for? What did you like about their management style?**

  This question has nothing to do with any of your former managers and everything to do with you. Your answer will indicate the type of environment you thrive in and where you might have some challenges. For example, if you say, *"My favorite manager was my old boss back when I worked at the pizza shop. We used to have so much fun hanging around the shop, playing video games and listening to music,"* well, it sounds fun, but doesn't say much about who you are or what you value in a leader or your work environment. Or maybe it does say something, but likely not what you want it to say.

  On the other hand, if your answer is something like *"The best manager I ever had was back when I first started my career as a help desk analyst. It was a scary time for me as a newcomer to the team, but I remember my manager always making herself available to answer any questions I had and really caring about my success as a member of her team."* In short, you've said you value leaders with engaging and supportive leadership styles.

- **How do you overcome objections when working with a difficult buyer?**

  In sales, objections become a regular part of the job. Think about it: your job is to convince the buyer; the buyer's job is to pick the right product or service for the job. They will ask lots of questions and won't always agree with your answers or approach. The interviewer is asking this question to validate your ability to navigate a challenging situation. Make sure your answer, which should be a real-life story, leaves them feeling confident in your ability to win over the buyer persona sometimes referred to as a blocker.

- **What is your role in a sales opportunity?**

  Show that you're all in and fully support the deal end to end. Some sales engineers are more engaged in supporting deals than others. The more you show you care, the better.

  Example: *"My role as the technical resource in the opportunity is to establish credibility and build trust with the appropriate stakeholders. Wherever possible, I build relationships that create additional paths to the win. My primary responsibility is to get the technical win, but I also support the opportunity through the sales win. If we don't get the sales win, the technical win doesn't matter as much."*

Interpersonal/communication skills

These questions usually aim to assess your ability to effectively communicate and build personal relationships. Be sure your answers reflect these skills. Some examples are provided here:

- **How would you approach explaining a complex concept to a non-technical audience?**

  When answering this question, it's important to demonstrate your ability to meet your audience at their level and speak their language. For example, your conversation style and talking points with a chief financial officer should be much different from those with a SOC analyst. It's helpful to use analogies and tell stories that simplify the concepts and make them relevant to your listener. Again, if possible, tell a story about a time you've actually done this.

- **Tell me about a time when you were able to convince a buyer to solve their problem in a different way.**

  Example: *"I remind myself going into every sales conversation that our buyers already have a picture of what they're looking for in mind and, most of the time, it looks nothing like what I have in my portfolio. This mentality prevents me from making assumptions and forces me to listen so I can visualize the buyer's desired outcome. In my experience, it's usually the process the buyer is highly opinionated about, so if I align with them on the desired outcome, I create the perception that we're in full agreement. This enables me to position my approach as a faster, more efficient path to the desired outcome instead of dismissing the buyer's thoughts on how things should be done. This approach has never failed me."*

- **How do you usually open your sales meetings?**

  Example: *"I like to open my sales calls with general conversation instead of getting down to business right away. Starting out this way encourages meeting attendees to let their guard down a bit and I'm often able to identify something we have in common so I can connect with them on a personal level."*

- **How do you decide what to include in your pitch or solution proposal?**

  Example: *"It's important to me to include enough detail in my presentation to address all the concerns and requirements of the buyer, but not more detail than necessary. Too much information can be confusing and open the door to unnecessary questions. After I've prepared my presentation, I put it through what I like to call the 'so what?' test. Anything in the presentation that doesn't have a specific purpose or add additional value gets removed."*

Sales skills

This area of the assessment is two-fold. On the one hand, the interviewer is seeking to validate your sales experience and your perspective on where your role as a sales engineer fits into the sales process. On the other hand, there is the very simple question – would I buy from you?

- **Describe your current sales process and your level of involvement.**

  This question separates good sales engineers from great ones. There is an implied question behind the stated question, and that is: are you truly a sales-focused technical resource, or are you a technical resource that supports the sales team upon request? You'd be surprised, but many sales engineers don't love the idea of being considered part of the sales team, so their approach is to parachute in to support sales requests, then parachute out. Great sales engineers see themselves as part of the sales team and remain engaged throughout the sales cycle. When you answer this question, you want to demonstrate your knowledge of a typical sales cycle and how you are able to influence opportunities at the various stages.

  Sales stages and definitions will vary from company to company, but a list of commonly used sales stages and high-level definitions is provided here:

  - **Lead generation** – Find potential buyers.

- **Qualification** – Determine whether the buyer is a good fit for your product or service.

- **Discovery** – Understand buyer challenges, pain points, timelines, requirements, and so on.

- **Proposal/presentation** – Present the proposed solution and pricing.

- **Evaluation/negotiation** – Buyer determines which vendor will be awarded their business.

- **Win/loss** – Opportunity is closed as a win or a loss.

Sales engineers can be involved at any of these stages but are most involved in the middle of the sales cycle, meaning they typically enter during or after *discovery*, and in most cases will own the presentation of the proposed solution (the sales rep will typically handle pricing), and participate in the *evaluation* process (PoV, competitive comparison, implementation requirements, and so on). Sales engineers want to achieve the technical win, meaning the buyer believes their solution is the best fit, but sales reps own the final commercial and legal negotiations that ultimately lead to the overall sales win or loss.

- **What is your definition of sales success?**

This is another question aimed at testing your sales IQ and level of buy-in as a member of the sales team. Articulate your understanding of the importance of the technical win, but also your awareness that the real success lies in the sales win. The sales win is how the sales team meets sales targets, retires quota, and earns commission – reiterate that you are a part of that team. Sales success should be rooted in financial goals, whether that's meeting quarterly or annual targets, driving $x\%$ in expansion opportunities, or growing your customer base by x number of new logos. At the end of the day, the goal is revenue generation, so make sure your answer aligns to that somehow. This is also a great opportunity to be seen as a team player.

- **How do you handle a situation where the solution you're selling may not be the best fit?**

  Hopefully, buyers that are not a good fit are disqualified during the *qualification* stage, which means a sales engineer would rarely encounter this situation. There are instances, however, where requirements are misunderstood, or a sales rep thinks there's a chance to win the business even though you may not agree. Remember, you're on the sales team, so your position should be to exhaust every option, including offering a solution that fits a subset of the requirements if you can't meet them all. Sales engineers are sometimes seen as a roadblock if they push too hard on requirements and introduce unnecessary friction. It's perfectly fine to stand your ground. You don't want to sell something that will lead to an unhappy customer, but you also don't want to appear inflexible during your interview. So, back to the main point, your answer should carry the theme of exhausting all options while maintaining the trust relationship and the integrity of the company. Who could be upset with that answer?

- **I'm a buyer that believes your solution is similar to a competitor's, and your solution is more expensive. Tell me why I should buy from you.**

  This is all about your ability to sell value. Don't make the mistake of focusing on features and functionality. Your buyer has clearly stated that their concern is price, which means you are very close to having the technical win – you just have to remind the buyer why you're better. To do this, remind them of why they began this journey in the first place. Remind them of the problem they're trying to solve and their desired outcomes, and why your solution gets them closer to that outcome, in a more effective, efficient, and sustainable way than the competition. Focus on the key differentiators, operational considerations, and competitor shortcomings that support your solution. Hopefully, at this point in the sales cycle, you know who the competitor is; if not, ask. If the buyer declines to tell you, see if they'll at least tell you what they like about the solution so you can provide an apples-to-apples comparison and highlight the pros and cons.

Technical skills

Technical skill requirements will vary based on the product or service you're selling. For example, if you are interviewing with an endpoint security vendor, you can expect questions to be focused on things such as operating systems, ransomware, policy management, and so on. The following questions are more generic in nature and focus more on your understanding of the product or service, your ability to position it, and your perspective on continuous learning:

- **How much do you know about what we do?**

    Do your homework. Learn as much as you can about the company's offering. Become familiar with the value proposition, key differentiators, integrations, top competitors: basically, whatever is publicly available to you. The way you answer this question shows the interviewer your level of interest, your ability to perform research and provide feedback, whether you understand the product or service offering, and ultimately, how steep your learning curve will be if you're hired.

- **Are you familiar with any of our competitor's offerings?**

    Again, *do your homework.* Know who the key competitors are and how the company you're interviewing with stacks up against them. Be prepared to identify ways you'd win against those competitors in a sales opportunity.

- **How do you stay up to date with the latest trends, breaches, and emerging threats?**

    Reference any blogs, articles, newsletters, podcasts, and so on that you leverage to stay in the know. If you attend conferences and webinars, highlight those as well. Depending on how you're feeling about the conversation, you could even bring up a recent noteworthy event, your thoughts on emerging threats and trends, or simply something you found interesting during your research. (You can expect to find sales engineers at well-known security conferences such as Black Hat and RSA, typically answering questions, providing demos, and delivering presentations at their company's booth.)

- **How do you keep your technical skills up to date?**

  Whether the role requires hand-on skills or not, understanding how things work only makes you better at your job. If you have a home lab, great! If you don't, be prepared to discuss other ways you prevent your skills from becoming outdated – even if it's reading whitepapers and watching video tutorials. This is important because even if you're not part of the implementation team, your buyers and their teams will want to understand the integration process and requirements, where applicable. The more you know and feel comfortable with, the more confident you will be in your sales conversations.

By no means is the list of questions included here intended to be exhaustive. As you prepare for interviews with specific organizations, ask yourself how these types of questions might show up in your interview and how the interviewer might ask them. The more you're prepared to tie your experiences to the specific needs of the company you're interviewing with, the more you'll stand out as a candidate. Remember, in a role like this, every call is a sales call – including the interview.

Summary

A career as a cybersecurity sales engineer can be incredibly lucrative and rewarding. The key to success is always seeking to understand the reason behind the question or concern, providing conversational answers and telling stories (avoiding binary answers where possible), and making sure your audience remembers you. Have fun in your interview – be yourself. Sure, the company you're interviewing with is assessing whether you're a good fit, but you should be doing that as well.

Finally, I'll leave you with this golden nugget…

Turn your interview into a conversation. There are only so many questions that can be asked in a 30-to-60-minute window. The more time you spend having a conversation, the more the interviewer gets to know you and remember you as a person, not just another candidate. Also (and this is super top-secret stuff!), conversations help limit the number of questions the interviewer can ask. Now, go out there and crush it!

In the next chapter, we'll pivot to the role of a CISO. This is actually great context for a cybersecurity sales engineer because many of your conversations will be with CISOs and other cybersecurity managers.

11
CISO

In this chapter, you will learn what a **chief information security officer (CISO)** is and the average salary range for this career in the US. Additionally, you will learn about the options for career progression and learn common interview questions for the role.

In this chapter, we will cover the following topics:

- What is a CISO?
- How much can you make in this career?
- What other careers can you do?
- Common interview questions for a CISO career

What is a CISO?

A CISO is a leader who is responsible for driving the information security program of an organization. Being a CISO is more than just understanding information security technologies and how the systems work together. It also involves understanding the business, including how the company operates, its regulatory and compliance environment, and its evolving external threat landscape.

As you can see, at this level in the organization, you require more than just technical expertise to be successful; you also need to have mastered working with the business and its different stakeholders, along with external parties from vendors to regulators.

The core aspect of any CISO's role is to shape the company's information security program. However, before you can do that, you must understand the organization's people, processes, and technology, and pair it with leadership, culture, and strategy. You need to be able to use this strategy to inform, communicate, and coordinate how you are going to achieve this across the different parts of the business.

How much can you make in this career?

The CISO compensation range greatly depends on the locality of the role, industry, and organization size. I have seen salaries ranging from $150,000 to $2.5+ million in total compensation, with many salaries averaging between $350,000 and $450,000. At this stage in your career, salaries start to separate into multiple buckets to include base compensation, bonuses, restricted stock units, company stock, and other items designed to tie compensation to the company's performance. Another form of payment is *vested* rewards such as stock or stock options, which are granted based on longevity with the company.

What other careers can you consider after becoming a CISO?

A career as a CISO means that you have mastered the ability to understand the business, its risk drivers, and its vulnerabilities, and you can design mitigation programs around it. CISOs have a broad offering of careers to consider, including board advisors, other CxO roles, consultancies, vCISOs (either virtual or fractional CISOs), and more. Sometimes, CISOs will leave their positions at mature companies and go back to start-ups as head of information security due to the potential upside of joining an early-stage start-up before it becomes public or acquired.

Common career questions for a CISO

The following is a list of interview questions that could prove useful in preparing for a CISO interview:

- **Why are you in cybersecurity?**

  While this might seem like a simple question, part of being at the leadership level is being able to easily communicate with stakeholders and other leaders who might not understand how these terms relate to them in the organization.

  Cybersecurity is the space of protecting organization assets (such as data, processes, and infrastructures) in digital form from unintended actions that affect the confidentiality, information, and integrity of those assets. It is often considered a subset of information security, which also includes the protection of information in analog form.

- **What is a threat and what is a risk?**

  A threat is something that has the potential to negatively impact an organization. These can range from a variety of different sources, including natural disasters (such as hurricanes, earthquakes, and floods), threat actors (an individual or group that wants to impose damage or harm to a person or organization), or other categories such as economic and regulator impacts to an organization. A risk is a function of that threat, exposure to that threat, the likelihood of occurrence, and any response or lack of response to the threat.

- **How do you measure risk as a CISO?**

  First, to be able to measure risk, you must be able to define it. Risk is the potential for something to affect an organization or business. This can be both positive and negative. Usually, risk is defined as a function of the potential impact of adverse events times the likelihood of that event. *Ryan Leirvik* mentioned in his book, *Understand, Manage, and Measure Cyber Risk*, that technology is inherently flawed because it is created by humans, and humans create technology.

I would like to make a calculation of risk from another field of study, as it is more inclusive of all the elements that we need to think about:

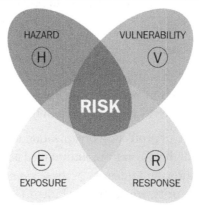

Figure 11.1 – Risk and it relations to its variables

A **vulnerability** in technology is the first element of risk that a CISO will measure. One of the ways to measure the size of a vulnerability is by using the **Common Vulnerability Scoring System (CVSS)** score (`https://nvd.nist.gov/vuln-metrics/cvss`). This uses **Common Vulnerabilities and Exposures (CVE)**, which is a list of publicly disclosed computer security flaws. The CVSS score uses several aspects of the vulnerability to produce a standardized score. Please refer to the CVSS calculator at `https://nvd.nist.gov/vuln-metrics/cvss/v3-calculator`. The following diagram shows the elements used to calculate it:

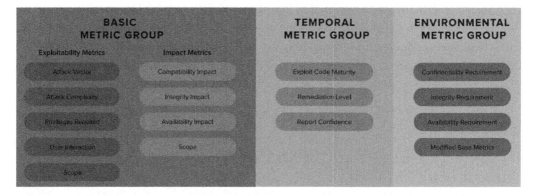

Figure 11.2 – CVSS score matrix (Source: `https://www.balbix.com/app/uploads/CVSS-Score-Metrics-Blog-e1592596353700.png`)

As a CISO, the vulnerability is just one aspect of the overall calculation; the threat of that vulnerability impacting the organization (or the **hazard**) or its likelihood of impacting the organization is next. As we translate this to cybersecurity, we need to think about how a vulnerability, which requires physical access, can only impact one machine and requires knowledge of the COBOL coding language. This might be something that occurs rarely and its impact might be limited. On the other end of this scale is a wormable vulnerability (this requires no human interaction), which is common on a majority of systems and allows threat actors to have full control of the machines. This has a high likelihood/impact rating. This is not world-ending as there are other aspects of the calculation that we can include:

Risk Rating Matirx

Impact	Likelihood				
	Rare	Unlikely	Possible	Likely	Almost certain
Catastrophic	moderate	moderate	high	critical	critical
Major	low	moderate	moderate	high	critical
Moderate	low	moderate	moderate	moderate	high
Minor	very low	low	moderate	moderate	moderate
Insignificant	very low	very low	low	low	moderate

Figure 11.3 – Risk rating matrix (Source: `https://focusergonomics.files.wordpress.com/2013/06/risk_matrix.jpg`

Exposure is the next aspect of that vulnerability that needs to be considered. For example, do you only have one secret server machine, which is not exposed to the internet, physical access, or connected to the network? This might be an offline machine host, with sensitive information such as crypto wallet keys or PKI root CA certificates. On the other end of the scale, there might be a vulnerability in the base image of your web hosts that are publicly exposed to the internet and scale to millions of machines to handle the increase in web traffic.

The final part of this risk calculation is your **response** to the situation. In terms of cybersecurity, this could be things such as compensating controls (for example, firewalls, network segmentation, hardening standards, and more), **incident response (IR)**plans to initiate additional changes, or control of the environment to minimize the effect on the environment. These actions will help reduce, minimize, or eliminate the vulnerability and/or any potential exposure to it.

This is just a simple way to calculate it, but these calculations and any corresponding monetary valuation of the risk will vary based on your knowledge of the environment, the assets, the impact on the business, and exposures.

- **How would you evaluate or develop a new security program at a new organization?**

    Your approach could be to use something such as a **strengths, weaknesses, opportunities, and threats (SWOT)** analysis or a threat model either at the organizational level or even at a particular departmental level. I would look at the organization starting with the business mission, understanding the people and processes currently in place from the business, and how they function to generate and produce results for the organization. Then, I would start to look at internal and external factors that could be a threat to those businesspeople/processes (these could range from inside threats to external threat actors or even regulatory and compliance). The following diagram is an example of a SWOT assessment that you might want to consider. In this case, we are considering whether the threat is internal/external to the organization and whether it might have a helpful or harmful impact on the organization:

Figure 11.4 – SWOT analysis example

The following diagram is an example of the outcome of a threat modeling exercise, where you would try to understand the potential threats that might face a specific application or service from an organization:

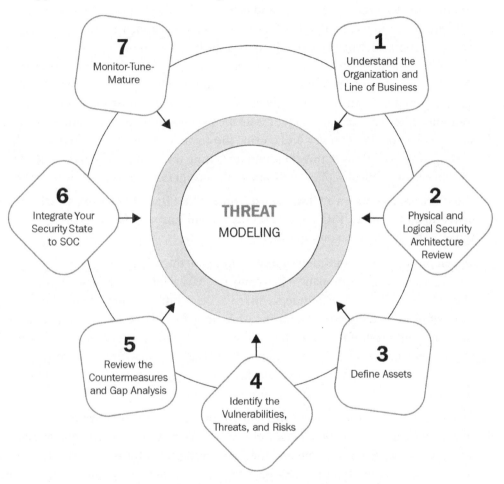

A Successful Threat Modeling Process

Figure 11.5 – Threat modeling framework

Before making any technology recommendations for your organizations, consider the existing technologies, current capabilities, and potential capabilities of additional modules, licenses, or features. Additionally, you can do a **return on investment (ROI)** assessment by adding a new solution to the organization or replacing the existing software with a unique solution. Do not forget to think about the people and processes, how these changes will affect them, and whether any user awareness or user training will be needed as a part of the modification process.

A significant part of the CISO's role is becoming a business enabler. It is not the goal of the CISO to implement security for the sake of security; it focuses on the business mission. As you think about implementing security technologies or solutions, you have to think about the people and processes involved, the risk that it helps mitigate, the residual risk that is left over, the user or customer friction introduced by the solution, and the value that it adds to the business in the long run. The value or ROI that the solution adds to the company must outweigh the user friction and your ability to mitigate risk to the business. Without this buy-in, end users in the company might not adopt or actively work to circumvent any of the implemented solutions. Alternatively, they might create the business case to their leaders that it is slowing them down too much and costing the business more money than the risk is mitigating. Situations at this stage end up getting resolved by the business leader with the most political capital and value to the business.

- **What are your views on a CISO focused on the first line of defense (security operations) versus a CISO focused on the second line of defense – GRC (governance, risk, and compliance)?**

Depending on the organization's business mission, the role of the CISO can differ. As a start-up, a company will usually not have a CISO as its first couple of employees. Usually, the founders will try to do as much as they can on their own before potentially hiring someone who can help them build the company's structure, and most of the time, they will start with IT first. The IT engineer might implement some security technologies to build the infrastructure. The growth continues; sometimes, their customers, their investors, or their industry start to require more structure around regulations and compliance.

As you can see, based on this growth path, in the beginning, organizations might start with CISOs with a GRC focus and a secondary focus on security operations. As the security program is built and the program matures, the direction of the CISO begins to shift away from the GRC focus toward starting to build out the rest of the security program, including operations (identification and detection), response, and recovery.

Once the program has been built, there is an ingrained conflict of interest regarding what prioritizes a security program – operations versus governance. This conflict of interest is very similar to IT versus security, where IT focuses on the availability of the equipment, and security is focused on the confidentiality of the program. In this case, GRC focuses on ensuring that the rules are followed, and there isn't too much risk, while operations are trying to collect signals and logs on the users, compute resources, and applications to ensure that there isn't any malicious activity. Sometimes, the amount of data being collected, the speed, or how things are being done in order to support the business might collect too much data in the logs or deploy things without following the policies and procedures. Once organizations get to this size or maturity, the CISO might be in charge of operations while reporting to a CIO/CEO or other CxO, and second-line functions such as GRC and audit might report to another CxO.

For more information on the security line of defense, please visit `https://www.isaca.org/resources/isaca-journal/issues/2018/volume-4/roles-of-three-lines-of-defense-for-information-security-and-governance`.

- **What are some of the cybersecurity frameworks that you're familiar with? Which one is your favorite and why?**

This helps you to show knowledge of the different frameworks within the industry, and whether you, as a candidate, are comfortable with one of the frameworks that the organization is already using. While it is not impossible to introduce a new framework to an organization, the time required to educate all the stakeholders on getting up to speed could potentially be spent elsewhere. One example is the NIST Cybersecurity Framework (`https://www.nist.gov/cyberframework`), which allows you to easily communicate what is needed to the leadership and acts as a Rosetta Stone to other commonly used frameworks such as the ISO 27001 (`https://www.iso.org/isoiec-27001-information-security.html`).

- **What are some of the key components that your third-party risk management program should address?**

Some of the key components that should be addressed are the products and systems (both off the shelf and open source), the custom applications built by the third party, the cloud services and shared responsibility, and the third-party consultants.

- **As a CISO, what are some ways that you can use to help map business goals to security decisions for a broad range of stakeholders?**

  Some of the techniques you can use are tabletop exercises around risk management, informal meetings, and enterprise architecture frameworks such as the Zachman Framework, the **Federal Enterprise Architecture Framework (FEAF)**, and **The Open Group Architecture Framework (TOGAF)**.

- **Tell me about a time when you had to modify an existing security policy and why you had to make the adjustment.**

  One example could be to determine that the current password policy of the organization did not require long, complex passwords. However, ultimately, this led to privilege escalation and lateral movement in a prior data breach. As the CISO, you then implemented a new policy that required long, complex passwords and that required the use of two-factor authentication, which helped mitigate future attacks.

- **Tell me about an audit you went through and the outcome.**

  Years ago, I worked in a consulting (virtual CISO) role at a healthcare organization that underwent an audit that discovered multiple vulnerabilities in the endpoints and some of the web servers. We identified that the critical vulnerabilities in the endpoints were caused by poor patch management and a lack of an antivirus solution. This was coupled with poor password management and open network shares of sensitive data. I worked with their team to implement new policies for passwords, change management, and data security. The network shares were locked down and sensitive data encrypted. The endpoints were also hardened against attacks. During a follow-up audit 6 weeks later, the auditors identified only a few minor security issues remaining.

- **Can you tell us about your leadership style?**

  For this question, the organization is assessing your capabilities to empower your team and delegate appropriately. The worst executive to hire is someone who wants to micromanage everything.

  Personally, I combine multiple leadership styles, such as coaching, delegation, visionary, servant, and being emotionally supportive. My approach focuses on setting a high-level objective for the team and then providing them with the space to be creative and play to their own strengths to meet or exceed the objective. I couple this with supporting the team as needed. The result of this approach has been team members who consistently exceed the **key performance indicators (KPIs)** and team members who have invented a new technology that has generated more revenue for the organization.

- **How do you handle situations where you have to tell someone "no," particularly when they don't report to you?**

One of the challenges of being a CISO is that, often, you need to be able to collaborate with stakeholders across the organization, some of whom might not be directly reporting to you. How you deal with these situations is a critical aspect of your ability to collaborate and resolve potential disagreements in differing approaches. Would you work through the *no* with that individual to understand their points of view? Would you escalate the situation to their peer on your level to influence them to have their stakeholder comply? Or would you potentially come to a compromise in approach with that stakeholder because it was the most efficient way to tackle the situation?

Rather than directly saying *"no"* as it relates to protecting the organization's risk, our compliance posture is saying *"while doing xxx seems like an effective approach, I would ask you to consider xxx."*

The only time I would say *"no"* is when something is deliberately unethical or illegal, and I would remove myself from the situation.

- **Can you share an experience where you had to collaborate with stakeholders across the organization to implement a security risk management program?**

This question is assessing your ability to successfully champion security initiatives across the organization.

An example for me is an organization I worked with that had suffered a ransomware attack. I was brought into the organization following the attack and worked with stakeholders across the organization to design, build, and implement a new security risk management program. Key parts of this new program included better detection and response of incidents, proactive security controls, an organization-wide security awareness training program, scheduled risk assessments, and new security policies. A key aspect of getting buy-in across the organization for this initiative was interviewing each stakeholder to identify what was critical to their team and then identifying the commonalities among teams, along with building out an implementation roadmap that implemented the most critical items first.

- **How do you train your teams?**

  Typically, I assess any skill gaps of my team members based on the role and the needs of the organization. Then, I schedule the more traditional training programs. In some instances, the team will need just-in-time training. For example, if a major ransomware attack hits the organization and it could have been detected and responded to faster, I will work to train the team in the latest detection and response best practices and work with them to identify any additional security controls that we could implement to protect against similar attacks in the future.

  As a CISO, I would also look to develop a pipeline of potential candidates who might be in different parts of the organization. Developing a security champion program helps you drive security awareness and drive the impact of your initiatives deeper into the organization. A by-product of this is that you now have individuals who are knowledgeable of the various lines of business and are also passionate about cybersecurity. Having security-related topics and training as part of the organizational budget versus department budgets also allows you to provide these security champions with training to help prepare them for potential roles in your organization.

- **Are there any new technologies that you plan to implement after coming on board this organization?**

  This is an open question that is used to determine your ability to think toward the future. For example, you might answer this question with something such as **artificial intelligence (AI)** and discuss how you plan to leverage AI capabilities to help improve the organization's security posture.

- **How would you describe a strong information security program?**

  A strong information security program is one that has a solid foundation of information security policies and procedures. Your information security program needs to align with the business objectives to empower the business and not block it from operations.

- **How do you measure the effectiveness of your information security program?**

  You should measure the effectiveness of your information security program by its ability to enable the business to improve productivity and security, without negatively impacting the business operations. For example, enable them to securely share information with clients, as it allows them to become more efficient in their communications to drive sales or customer retention. If the program is being measured in terms of effectiveness, I maintain a scorecard to track it. In a large enterprise, it is important to measure and communicate the effectiveness of programs. Additionally, I use metrics and dashboards that are easy for executives to quickly read.

- **Let's say you find a development team has numerous unpatched vulnerabilities that are considered high risk. How would you influence those individuals to remediate those vulnerabilities? ~ Ross Young**

  This question focuses on your ability to influence individuals who are outside your control while also doing it without using authority as a potential driver unless absolutely necessary. You should be able to show those outside the organization why something might be important to them and, in turn, impact the organization. Additionally, you should be able to demonstrate to them why resolving it on their own would be more efficient than letting it wait until later.

- **Do you think the size of an organization affects whether security should be outsourced?**

  Yes; it often costs less to outsource security to a **managed security services provider** (**MSSP**) that already has the in-house talent than it is to try and hire full-time employees into a smaller organization. The other advantage of outsourcing is the ability to pull in different specialties when you need them. For example, if you need specialists that can conduct advanced malware analysis, it is usually more cost-effective to leverage the existing talent in your third-party service provider.

  Larger organizations also outsource, but often, they will have internal security teams.

- **Tell me about a top executive decision you have made in the past, the circumstances around the decision, and the outcome of that decision.**

  As an executive, I had to determine the best way to continue scaling the organization while needing to reduce the department's overall spending. I made the difficult decision to remove some of the contract workers we had and temporarily spread their workload around, including assigning some to myself, for a short period of time.

- **Can you describe zero trust to a non-technical stakeholder?**

  Zero trust is a concept that assumes attackers are already within your network and endpoints. To explain this to a child (or a non-technical stakeholder), I would mention it in the old way of thinking, "Would you trust me with all of your candy because your mom let me in the house?" I would then explain the risk associated with this is that I might take all of your candy and not give you any of it. With zero trust, even though your mom let me inside the house, you would still ask me questions before allowing me access to any candy, and you would have each type of candy segmented from the other types, so I would be unable to get all of your candy in one try.

- **How does compliance affect your decision-making process?**

  Compliance will drive the security program for the organization based on the industry. For example, if the organization is in healthcare, the **Health Insurance Portability and Accountability Act (HIPAA)** of 1996, the **Health Information Technology for Economic and Clinical Health (HITECH)** Act, which was enacted as part of the American Recovery and Reinvestment Act of 2009, and the **Health Information Trust (HITRUST)** Alliance are key considerations for compliance, which we will need to address across the organization.

- **What do you define as the key attributes every CISO should have?**

  Some of the key attributes I think every CISO should have are effective communication skills, adaptability, effective negotiation skills, active listening skills, and the ability to collaborate effectively with other stakeholders across the organization.

- **Give me an example of how you balance the cost of your information security program.**

  Typically, I start with the available budget, review the security controls we need to implement, work with the team to identify the higher-priced options and cost-effective options for controls, and then consider the value of each solution. We conduct a trade-off analysis to determine what we can implement and through what period of time.

  Additionally, by tying the security program to business enablement, we can work with other lines of business/departments to enable their own initiatives through the security program and have them sponsor a part of the budget for their solutions.

- **What do you see as some of the emerging risks that enterprises will face?**

  At the time of writing, some of the emerging risks that enterprises will face include the increased use of AI in attacks, the increase in ransomware-as-a-service operators, the increase of cybersecurity insurance policy premiums or the lack of insurability, quantum computing and its ability to break current encryption algorithms, and cybersecurity attacks from space assets.

- **How would you handle a situation in which all your critical systems have been encrypted by a group of hackers? Describe the steps and decisions that need to be made.**

  Firstly, I wanted to recommend remaining calm in situations such as this to ensure that you are properly considering all the aspects of the situation. I would recommend that I let the system owners verify the health of all the mentioned systems to see how they might be potentially impacted. It should be pretty obvious if the machines or storage systems of these systems are encrypted.

  If something seems off, it is time to spin up an investigation team, to start gauging the extent of the event. Then, I would start working with the security team to potentially look at the **indicators of attack (IOAs)**, as well as bringing in threat intelligence to start validating chatter that might be on the internet. As the teams start to potentially discover **indicators of compromise (IOCs)**, you will need to start assessing the severity of the potential incident. (More information about IOAs versus IOCs can be found at `https://www.crowdstrike.com/cybersecurity-101/indicators-of-compromise/ioa-vs-ioc/`.)

  Once you have declared the incident, you will want to bring out the **IR** plan to be able to communicate the status to the business and respond to the incident. Hopefully, at this point, there is a well-defined and tested IR plan. The detection and analysis have already started with the IOAs and IOCs. The next phase would, typically, be focused on the containment and rededication phase. You would not want the threat to spread to other systems to cripple the organization further. This containment and rededication should block off communication to these infected systems. **Digital Forensics Incident Responders (DFIR)** should clone images from these infected systems to start the DFIR investigation process. Part of any IR plan is to ensure that you are able to continually update business leaders, which might include legal and public relations, on the status of the situation.

Backup and restore is likely the next phase of the response. One of the challenges with the backup and restore phases is that many companies only end up doing backups or partial restores. Often, the complexities of backing up and restoring prevent companies from completely validating the backup and restore. Once you have contained the incident within your system, you should start the restore process.

One of the challenges is that threat actors are aware of this process and have now started to target backup processes in order to corrupt or delete backups.

If the backups are unaffected, you should choose the last authentic backup and start the restore process. Once the restore is completed, you should validate that there are no IOCs in the newly restored system. Additionally, the business will also need to validate the restore to ensure that business functionality is fully restored.

Lastly, it is recommended that a post-mortem is conducted so that the teams can learn lessons from the incident. This helps them to update their system configurations regarding detection, IR, backup, and restore and recovery.

- **How do you communicate the business impact of a breach to other executives? Focus on cost and the cost of solutions to mitigate in the future.**

  In my experience, cost and compliance are the two main areas of focus. I focus on the cost of the attack or breach, followed by the cost of solutions to mitigate a similar attack in the future, and finally, the compliance concerns the organization has.

  Another approach you can take is to align your security program to the business mission and demonstrate how security helps drive business revenue. For example, if a particular attestation or resiliency capability can drive sales or customer retention, work with business leaders to demonstrate that ROI.

- **How do you empower members of your team in their cybersecurity careers?**

  I meet with each team member to identify their short- and long-term goals and then identify how I can help each of them within the allotted budget to grow their career.

  Using their career drivers, I can work to assign them to projects that align with their career interests and organizational needs. Providing them with ownership over these initiatives allows them to grow in those areas, and they are likely to deliver more value than if they were just assigned to them as part of their role and be of no interest to them.

- **How do you balance risk to the business and security controls?**

  I balance the risks to the business and security control implementation by conducting a trade-off analysis of the risk to the daily business operations of each security control and the risk of not implementing those security controls.

- **How do you stay current on legislation that may affect the organization's security initiatives?**

  In order to stay current on the legislation that might affect the organization's security strategy, I create Google alerts and monitor **Really Simple Syndication (RSS)** feeds for these topics to ensure that I can see when they are being introduced and the progress they make.

- **What would you implement to manage endpoints on the network that do not meet minimum security requirements?**

  An overarching answer here would be zero trust, but specifically, you could use something such as a **network access control (NAC)** policy that blocks devices from the network that do not meet minimum security requirements.

- **You are the new CISO for a healthcare organization and need to review the policies and procedures of the organization to ensure the organization is compliant with HIPAA and other healthcare laws. What type of security assessment would you perform?**

  In this situation, you would perform a regulatory compliance assessment.

- **What is your elevator pitch?**

  Everyone needs to be able to summarize the value that they would bring to an organization in a maximum of one or two sentences. For example, mine is "I translate between people and processes and the technology that helps enable those business missions. I use a consultative and coaching approach to drive overall cybersecurity maturity, the strategy needed, and the people development that achieves organizational success."

As you can see, the role of a CISO can vary dramatically from needing to be tactical regarding the different technical threats that an organization might face to being able to interact and help enable the business mission with counterparts in different departments. The CISO needs to have a varying balance of hard and soft skills in order to be successful in their role.

Summary

In this chapter, you learned what a CISO is, the average salaries in the US for a CISO, and common questions you might be asked during an interview.

In the next chapter, you will learn some of the most common behavioral interview questions that are asked in these interviews.

12
Behavioral Interview Questions

This chapter covers some of the most common behavioral interview questions. These questions are grouped by category, and they help employers to assess a candidate's soft skills. You can benefit from learning these questions and practicing their responses, as I have experienced many of these questions being asked in cybersecurity interviews verbatim.

In this chapter, the following topics will be covered:

- Why are behavioral questions asked in an interview?
- Common behavioral interview questions

Why are behavioral interview questions asked in an interview?

Behavioral interview questions are asked to help the interviewer gain insight into how you have handled past situations at work, which can help them see how you might handle similar situations in their company.

Many behavioral interview questions you are asked in interviews start with phrases similar to the following:

- Describe a situation where you…

- How did you handle [situation]…?

- Give me an example of…

- Tell me about a time when you…

Before going into an interview, I suggest you review the job posting and identify the keywords that the employer is listing. This can help you tailor your answers to behavioral interview questions by using some of the keywords from the job description. Also, I recommend doing a self-assessment to identify 5–10 key skills that you have, and then identify situations where you have used those skills. For example, perhaps you are a good communicator, and you can identify that you used your communication skills to diffuse a difficult situation at a previous job. That is an example you can use to answer one of the behavioral interview questions.

When answering behavioral interview questions, I recommend you use something such as the **S.T.A.R.** technique, which stands for **situation**, **task**, **action**, and **result**.

For the situation strand, you want to describe the situation you were in and set the scene for the interviewer. For the task strand, describe the issue or situation that you were confronted with. For action, describe the intervention or action you did in the situation. And, finally, for the result strand, tell the interviewer how your actions solved the problem and how you helped the company. When you answer, try to be clear and concise and use quantifiable results wherever possible. For example, your action during the situation might have resulted in a 20 percent reduction in IT support tickets, so be sure to mention this fact to the interviewer.

Common behavioral interview questions

Behavioral questions assess a variety of areas to see how you function in a company and contribute to the success of both your team and the organization. I want to stress that your answers to these questions do not have to be targeted toward cybersecurity or IT jobs. Any situation you have experienced in the past could be used to answer these questions. If you find that you do not have past experience that is applicable to a question, inform the interviewer and answer with what you would do if confronted with the scenario presented by the interviewer.

For each of the following questions, I will provide an example of how I would answer the question based on my own experience or a fictional situation.

Adaptability

The following questions are designed to assess your adaptability to changing situations in the workplace:

- **Can you describe a major change at a company you worked at and how you handled this change?**

  An example of this was when I worked as a laundry washer in a hospital laundry facility and the dryers caught on fire and shut down. This meant I could not wash any of the laundry loads. However, the trucks delivering the loads from the surrounding hospitals did not stop, so the entire back area of the building was filled with dirty laundry. I quickly volunteered with the maintenance team to help them replace parts in the dryers so that they could work again. It took a few days of non-stop washing and some late hours, but we ultimately worked through the backlog of laundry.

- **Can you tell me about a situation in which you had to adjust to changes over which you had no control and how you handled the situation?**

  An example of this is when I worked in healthcare, and the company I worked for closed one of its divisions and laid off everyone. I found out on a Friday that, effective Monday morning, I would be unemployed. So, I identified any openings in the division of the company that was still open and spoke with the management team there to determine whether I was a good fit. Ultimately, I decided to move to another company, but it was important for me to take action and not just wait to be rescued.

- **Can you tell me about a time when you had to adapt to a difficult situation?**

  Back when I worked as a nurse, I worked in some bad neighborhoods, and in one case, there was a homicide near my car. I had to adapt by getting into the vehicle through the passenger side and navigating the slew of emergency vehicles and crime scene tape in the area.

- **What do you do when your priorities need to change quickly? Can you provide an example?**

  I adapt and re-prioritize. One example is when, years ago, I was working on a marketing project for a client. After performing most of the work, the client determined that they wanted to pivot their marketing, which typically would have required a few weeks of extra work to rebuild the funnels. I listened to the stakeholders to identify their rationale for the change, made the requested pivot, and worked quickly to perform the rebuild in a few days. The ultimate result for the client was an increase in revenue with the new marketing campaign.

Ambitiousness

The following questions are intended to assess your level of ambition:

- **Can you tell me about a project you worked on that was your idea and where you led the implementation?**

  I worked at a help desk for a healthcare organization and was tired of receiving support calls about a piece of supply chain management software every single time nurses wanted to order more supplies. The main issue was that the training from the vendor was horrible, so none of the nurses wanted to watch it. Instead, they relied on me to walk them through ordering each time they needed supplies. I built a suggested training program and presented it to executive management, showing the cost savings of just having me train everyone versus relying on vendor training. Management agreed, and I rolled out the program that helped reduce our support calls by about 22 percent.

- **Can you tell me about a time when you made a suggestion to improve the work in your organization?**

I worked for a janitorial company and noticed that the cleaning route they had me follow was causing me to drive miles out of my way each night, which led to an increase in gas costs and my travel miles. I spoke with customers on my route and asked if they minded me shifting their cleaning hours to adjust my route for optimal time management. The clients liked my idea because it meant their establishments would be cleaned earlier in the evening, and it meant I could spend more time in each business to ensure a deep clean instead of the high-level cleaning they were paying for. I then presented the idea to my boss, mentioned clients were on board with the idea, and it was approved.

- **Describe an important goal you set in the past and how you reached it.**

One example is getting my undergraduate degree. A few weeks after starting the program, my spouse had emergency surgery, and at the halfway mark of the first semester, I had a failing grade. I met with the school dean who challenged me to finish the semester with a passing score. I completed the missing assignments and extra credit to end up with a perfect (4.0) GPA that semester, winning awards from the university for my grades.

- **Describe two examples from previous jobs or life experiences that show you are willing to work hard.**

I worked for an EdTech company building courses. A client requested an urgent course, so I spent the weekend filming and editing the entire course for the client to have it the following Monday. This required me to skip sleep for the entire weekend. The end result was that the client loved the training and appreciated the fast delivery.

Another example is when I was in the military. I had some injuries, including a hole in my foot, right before a road march to complete the qualification for one of my training schools. Instead of taking the option to recycle to another training class and heal my wounds, I instead ran the entire road march to finish at the front of the unit while ignoring the pain of my injuries.

- **What were your study patterns in school? And how many hours do you spend working each day?**

  In school, I found I could always learn information faster than others, so I would spend my free time continuing to learn the next level of any subject area. Because of my military background, I only sleep a few hours each day, which opens up time to complete any tasks. I always liked the quote from the movie *Shawshank Redemption*: "Get busy living or get busy dying." I choose to live every day.

- **Describe a time when you had to go above and beyond the call of duty in order to get a job done.**

  As a pediatric nurse, I had a patient (a 6-month-old baby) who was under critical care in his home. One day, a few minutes before my shift ended, the baby had an episode where he stopped breathing and had to be resuscitated. The ambulance arrived to take the child to the hospital, but instead of packing up and going home, I went with the child and his family to the hospital to make sure there were no issues on the way since the **Emergency Medical Technicians (EMTs)** arriving on the scene did not have experience with ventilators. The baby ended up surviving the experience and is now a healthy teenager.

- **Can you tell me about a challenging time at your workplace when a job or task had to be completed? How you were able to focus on completing the job or task?**

  When I worked as a pediatric nurse, I walked into my shift to find a child's ventilator alarm ringing and the child blue in the face. The nurse on duty was holding the child and telling me that the child was just a little fussy. I could immediately tell the child had an issue with his airway. I took the child from the other nurse and assessed his airway to find that his trach (a breathing tube) had been removed and the child could not breathe. While that nurse was yelling at me that nothing was wrong with the baby and the mom who had just entered the room was screaming and crying, I was laser-focused on changing the trach and establishing an airway for the child so that he could breathe. I changed the trach within seconds and used an Ambu bag (the same bag that paramedics use in Hollywood movies to help a patient breathe) to deliver oxygen to the baby. The baby's skin color improved, and he was able to breathe normally.

- **Can you tell me about a time when you were effective in prioritizing tasks and completing a project on schedule and within budget?**

I led a project where the company was developing proprietary software for patient case management. The initial scope of the alpha version of the project was a barebone functionality that would be deployed to a single team. Once other teams started providing input on the project, we started seeing a large amount of scope creep. I called a meeting with each department's management team and worked with them to identify what was absolutely crucial for a core solution across all departments and what the individual department needs were. Then, our team focused on implementing the core items that the other teams deemed critical. I gained stakeholder buy-in for this plan from all department heads. The end result was that we delivered the alpha version of the project 3 weeks early and were under the planned budget.

- **Describe a project you had that demanded a lot of initiative from you.**

I started a new job at a healthcare company, which used an old electronic medical records system. Their main issue was the company that developed the software was no longer in business and no one at the healthcare company had been trained by the vendor to use the software. My boss told me I needed to train the nursing staff on the system and show them how to use new features. I took the initiative and read through the engineering manuals from the vendor and also scoured the internet to find any information regarding the software. The end result was not only being able to train staff effectively, but I also identified ways the software could be used more efficiently, which led to time being saved for producing nursing documentation and a greater ability to pull critical data from the system to help physicians.

- **How do you stay current with industry trends, new technology, and your skills?**

For me, I stay current by investing in myself in the form of courses, books, and conferences. I have found one of the best ways to truly know you have a skill is to be able to teach it to others.

- **Describe a time you worked without close supervision and the result.**

I worked at a company that had created the position for me, so my boss didn't fully understand what someone in the job role could do. She left me alone after my first day and assumed I would just be completing the required training from human resources. Instead, I completed all of that training within a few hours and started fielding calls from nursing staff to help them with technical issues. I also implemented a reconciliation process that saved the company tens of thousands of dollars each month.

- **What impact did you have at your last job?**

I helped grow revenue and improve client satisfaction.

What you might notice with this answer is how I kept it brief and direct to answer the question. An interviewer would then typically ask you to expand upon your first answer with additional information about how you helped grow revenue or improve client satisfaction. Remember, for some questions, you just want to give the interviewer the bare minimum answer and allow them to start digging deeper.

- **What was the most competitive work situation you have experienced? And how did you handle it?**

For me, it was during the military. Many people were trying to do the same job role I wanted to do. So, I focused on a self-assessment to identify my strengths and weaknesses, and then I focused all of my efforts on maximizing my strengths. This led to me passing difficult training schools that others, who were more qualified on paper, failed.

- **Describe a risky decision you made and the outcome.**

I applied for an IT internship in another state and used my remaining dollars to buy a round-trip ticket. At the time, I had not used a computer much and didn't know anything about computer networking, so I purchased a book on networking and read through it on the plane ride to the other state. I was able to talk my way through the interview and then worked hard over the next few weeks on the job to build my networking skills. The outcome was that I was offered a full-time job with the company after just 2 weeks.

- **Describe some challenges you faced in your last job and how you handled them.**

One challenge in my last role was that the team was spread across different countries and time zones. I handled this challenge by encouraging flexibility in meetings and only holding meetings that were directly related to executing on a project. Any meetings that were being held for brainstorming were limited as well.

Another challenge was that some members of leadership had personal agendas, and so having to navigate those to push projects forward. A key way of handling this was to identify each agenda and discern what was truly critical to that person and what was a nice-to-have item on their list.

- **Are there projects that you have started on your own recently? And what caused you to start them?**

A recent project of mine is writing a book. I started this project so that I could give back to the cyber community by sharing the knowledge I have collected over the years.

- **Describe some things you have done to invest in yourself and improve your skills.**

Each year, I set aside a budget to invest in courses, books, coaching, and conferences.

- **Can you tell me about an idea that you came up with during your career and how you applied it?**

When I worked as a nurse, I invented a medical device out of necessity to make my job easier. I ended up pursuing a provisional patent application and selling the rights of the device to a large healthcare company that made a competing product.

- **How do you handle disagreements with your management team?**

I simply follow a process of allowing the other person to share their point of view and ask questions with an open mind. Often, I find that the other person in management has more contextual information than I do, which allows them to take a more well-informed position on the subject.

- **If you have several projects you need to do, how do you prioritize getting everything done?**

I follow the same process for work as I do for life, which is the ABC method. The "A" tasks are those that are absolutely critical to get done today or this week and have the maximum impact on the organization. Usually, completing these tasks helps you complete the "B" and "C" tasks, too. The "B" tasks are those that would be nice to get done today or this week, but they can be moved to the following week. The "C" tasks are the nice-to-have tasks that have minimal impact on the organization.

Analytical thinking

The following questions are designed to test your analytical thinking skills:

- **Can you provide an example of how you use your analytical abilities?**

  As an executive, I have to analyze problems and identify which main problem I can solve that removes many of the smaller problems I encounter. For example, learners might experience issues with an individual lab assignment, which is a small problem. If they experience issues with several labs, this becomes a larger problem, and the solution might be to switch to another lab provider.

- **Developing and using a detailed procedure is important in a job. Tell me about a time when you had to develop and use a procedure to successfully complete a project.**

  As a pediatric nurse, a challenge that I faced was bath time with the babies because they would try to pull out their trach (used for an airway to breathe) and feeding tubes. I developed a process to bathe a child by distracting them with a pile of toys I had stashed nearby while keeping the baby from pulling out its trach and feeding tube.

- **Can you walk me through your decision-making process?**

  For decision-making, I always think about the impact my decision will have in the future. For example, if I need to approve or disapprove budget expansion on a project, I review how the project will impact the company over the next 3–5 years. If the project will drive more revenue in the next 3–5 years, I don't mind increasing the short-term expenditure.

  Another key to any decision-making process is to ensure you have adequate sleep, eat properly, and remove yourself emotionally from the decision.

- **Please provide an example of a time when you used good judgment and logic to solve a problem.**

  One night as a pediatric nurse, I noticed that my patient seemed very excited. From my experience, I knew babies typically became excited like that if they were either using the restroom or if their airway was compromised. I trusted my judgment and checked the child's airway to discover that their trach tube had been pulled out. I quickly changed to a new tube and re-established their airway.

- **Provide an example of when you took a risk to achieve a goal. What was the outcome?**

  After being homeless and hungry, I decided to bet on myself and went to a local military recruiting station to enlist. At that point in my life, I had never left my local area, but I decided to take the chance. That decision helped me get a steady paycheck and a place to live, which helped propel me in my career and life.

- **Can you give an example of when using precision was critical for your job?**

  In the military, my shots had to be on target when clearing buildings; otherwise, my teammates could be injured or killed by my rounds (during live-fire training). I chose to spend extra hours practicing my craft to reduce the likelihood that I would cause harm to my team.

- **Tell me about a time when you had to analyze information and make a recommendation.**

  As an executive, I analyze information and have to make a decision within minutes based on the available data. An example of this is when I had a demonstration from a new lab provider and had to decide either yes or no on moving forward with them based on this short demonstration.

- **Can you give me an example of when you had to have attention to detail to complete a task successfully?**

  In military training, we were assigned random cleaning tasks in the barracks. My responsibility was to clean a drinking fountain so that it would shine. Unlike others in the barracks, I would take my time on the drinking fountain to remove all of the water spots and would guard the drinking fountain until the instructors came in to complete the inspection. All of the instructors commented how the drinking fountain I was responsible for was cleaner than the water in the Caribbean.

Building relationships

The following questions are designed to see your effectiveness at building relationships:

- **Give an example of a time when you had to address an angry customer and diffuse the situation.**

  Back when I worked at a fast-food restaurant, I had a customer screaming and cursing me because their $0.99 breakfast sandwiches included a charge for sales tax, which was required by law. The customer had ordered 20 sandwiches but only had $20 on them. With tax, their total came to $21. After getting approval from my manager, I simply asked the customer if they would be willing to part with one breakfast sandwich to reduce the order to under $20 in exchange for getting 3 free hash browns and orange juice. The customer agreed to this and left. A few months later, I ran into that same customer again and he apologized for his behavior that day.

- **Can you tell me about a time when you were not able to build a relationship with someone because they were too difficult to deal with?**

  During a business transaction, I had someone who did not hold up their end of the deal. I attempted to work with this person and extended many deadlines over the course of a year. Ultimately, I made the decision to just cut ties with this person and take the financial loss because the time investment was costing me more money. Shortly thereafter, my business accelerated even more, while their business went under.

- **Tell me about a time when you had to quickly establish rapport under difficult conditions.**

  In the military, we had a short period of time on patrol to establish positive relations with locals. I used the simple psychology of smiling and waving at people and just treating them as equals, which helped us get intelligence on our adversaries.

- **What do you think are the keys to establishing successful business relationships? And can you provide an example of how you used them in your life?**

  Relationships are the currency of life. In business, the key is to always focus on the other party's needs. If you deliver value to the marketplace, then the marketplace will tell everyone else about you, so you will never need to spend money on advertising. By establishing successful business relationships, I have been able to make a phone call or send a text message to get people hired into cybersecurity jobs after those people had been applying for jobs for over a year. In one case, a young woman was able to get a job offer within 2 hours of me calling someone, and she started work the next day.

Business systems thinking

The following questions are designed to assess whether you have big-picture thinking and how you navigate office politics:

- **Describe how your position contributes to the company's overall objectives.**

  In one of my current roles, I am an executive. My position directly contributes to the core of the business, which is training, along with the overall strategic objective of scalability.

- **Are you a big-picture person or more detail-oriented?**

  I am a combination of both. I always think strategically over the long term and focus on attention to detail to deliver quality outcomes.

- **Have you experienced a politically complex situation at work? If yes, please describe it and how you came to a positive outcome.**

  Typically, I remain out of office politics, since I focus on being productive. There was an incident where two women were in a fistfight in the office, and I was called in to give my version of events. However, since I kept to myself, I actually didn't know they fought until I was called into the office, so I had no additional context to provide my boss. The ultimate outcome of this was that one woman was fired immediately and the other was fired a few weeks later.

Caution

The following questions are designed to assess your ability to use caution when guidelines are not clear and to exercise caution against burnout by performing a self-assessment:

- **Have you ever worked in a situation where the rules and guidelines were not clear? How did it make you feel?**

  I have been in many work situations where instructions were lacking. In one case, I worked as a nurse in an elderly nursing home as a contractor. When I arrived for my shift, the outgoing nurse didn't give me a report (which was required under law at the time), and the paperwork for the patient charts and medication delivery was terrible. Coupled with all of this, I had over 70 patients to care for that night, since another nurse called in sick. I had to quickly look through the paperwork on the facility policies and procedures to determine what I needed to do and read through the physician notes to determine what medications the patients needed. I was able to successfully complete the shift, but the outcome was that I never went back to that facility and transitioned into pediatric nursing.

- **Can you tell me about a time when you demonstrated too much initiative on a project?**

  One time I demonstrated too much initiative on a project was when I built a large number of custom labs for a client almost 3 months prior to their expected deadline because I worked 20-hour days and 7 days a week to finish. The downside of this was the client then expected future labs to be delivered on a similar timeline, which I did, but it was not a sustainable business model in the long term.

Communication

The following questions are designed to assess your communication skills:

- **Can you tell me about a situation where you were able to effectively "read" another person and tailor your actions to your understanding of that person's needs?**

  One time, I was delivering a speech and was able to read the audience to tell the children were getting bored with the topic. So, I adjusted my approach and explained the topic in the context of a video game they might play, which captured their attention.

- **Can you share an experience where you didn't feel like you communicated effectively? What happened and how did you resolve the situation**

- I had expectations for my team members to complete a project by a specific deadline. I noticed that there was little production on the project and it was getting close to the deadline. When I asked the team members if they needed help, I was always met with a no. Finally, I asked whether any of them understood the ultimate business objective of this project and none of them did. By explaining what we were trying to do, the team members felt more conviction about seeing the project completed, and we were able to complete the project on time and under budget.

- **How have you used effective communication to strengthen a relationship?**

  As a nurse, I had a co-worker who didn't like me because of my race. She assumed that because we were in the South, all people of my race must be terrible. One day, I was tired of her microaggressions, so I sat down with her, addressed my concerns, and asked her to share about how she grew up. Additionally, I shared my upbringing in the North, swapping stories of crazy patients we both had at other companies. As soon as she found out I was not born in a Southern state, she treated me with respect and we had no further issues.

- **How would you communicate a difficult or unpleasant idea to your manager**

- The first thing I would do is perform a trade-off analysis of either decision. This means I would determine what the benefits and drawbacks would be to the manager saying yes versus the benefits and drawbacks to the manager rejecting my idea. My next step would be to determine any objections the manager might have to the idea and identify a response to each objection.

- **What is the most important presentation you have completed?**

  I created a presentation to help minority and veteran small business owners in my local city identify cybersecurity best practices that they could implement on a tight budget, which would significantly help reduce risks for their businesses.

- **Can you give an example of how you successfully communicated with someone who didn't like you or who you didn't like?**

  There was a manager from another department who didn't like me for unknown reasons. I simply approached this individual with respect each time, even though they were rude to me, and kept the conversation focused on the task at hand and not personal things.

- **Describe a time you had to sell an idea to your co-workers or a manager. What was your process? And were you successful in selling the idea?**

One time I had to sell managers of other departments an idea to create a training program across the company. Before pitching the idea, I put myself in the other manager's shoes to determine what might be important to them and any objections they might have to the proposal. I then presented my idea to the first group of managers and adjusted my presentation for additional managers based on any additional objections to the idea, so I could move the project forward. Ultimately, I was able to get buy-in from all departments on the project, and we were able to roll out the training program successfully, which saved the company a significant amount of money over the next several years.

- **How do you communicate critical information to your team?**

The communication style varies between email, a meeting, or some other form of communication, but my process is the same. I always focus on the end objective that we want to accomplish and focus on how the change or idea will impact the daily workflow of my team. Then, I convey the information in a transparent manner and answer any questions around it. If I identify that several team members are asking similar questions, I create a job aid reference for the team to answer some of the common questions.

- **How do you keep your manager informed about your work?**

In the past, I would typically have a weekly meeting to check in with management on projects and any blockers I was facing. As an executive, my life is full of meetings, so check-ins with other executives happen on a daily basis.

- **How do you explain complex technical topics to non-technical stakeholders?**

I always relate the technical topic to something from everyday life that the person is familiar with either because they have experienced it themselves or because they have seen it in a movie or a television show. For example, years ago, I began working at a company where the nursing staff was resistant to cybersecurity training. Having been a nurse in a previous life, when I came on board, I decided to relate the training objectives to things a nurse would care about. In one instance, the objective was to not share your login credentials with other nurses, which was a huge issue at this company.

During training, I asked the nurses if any of them wanted to keep their nursing licenses and everyone raised their hands. Then, I asked whether any of them wanted to redo their nursing charting on patients at the end of each day. None of the hands in the room were raised. Next, I asked for two volunteers and ran through a scenario where a regulatory agency came in for an audit and found one nurse documenting but another's nurse's name being signed on the nursing note. I asked both nurses whether they wanted someone else's name to be signed on their nursing notes. Of course, the answer was no. I then explained how sharing their login credentials for the **electronic medical record** (**EMR**) system would lead to the name of the nurse logged in to be signed on every note and that this was the reason we didn't want them sharing login credentials with each other. After this training, the company was able to see a significant reduction in credential sharing among nursing staff.

- **What types of communication situations cause you difficulty? Please provide an example.**

As an introvert, public speaking has always been a challenge for me because I would prefer to sit quietly in the back of the room. My way around this was to practice giving speeches in front of the mirror and giving speeches to my cat. She didn't care about what I had to say by the way. But by practicing an area I considered a weakness, I became more comfortable when put in uncomfortable situations.

- **Tell me about a time you did a successful speech. How did you prepare for it?**

A few years ago, I presented a webinar to several thousand business owners. I prepared for this webinar by selecting a topic that many business owners would care about, which was how to improve their marketing campaigns and sales conversions on a low budget. I then sent out a survey to business owners that I knew to identify some of the challenges they were facing in this area. My next step was to identify solutions to those issues, and then I created my slides for the presentation. A key component of my presentation was case studies across industries, where the business owners experienced challenges that had surfaced in that survey. The end result of the presentation was helping business owners and increasing my own client list.

- **Describe a time you had a conflict with your supervisor and how you handled it.**

  I had a supervisor once that played with puppets most of the day, and she used to have the puppets peer around the corner of the wall at me to ask me questions. This led to me surfacing my concerns with the puppets each day to her and her yelling at me that there was nothing wrong with the puppets. Finally, I approached her and asked if a customer came in and witnessed puppets peering around the corner talking to them, what did she think they would say and who would they say it to? She mentioned that they would not like it and they would report it to her manager. Once she was able to see the issue from the customer's point of view, the puppet issue cleared up.

- **Can you tell me about a time you had to present complex information? How did you assess that your audience retained the information?**

  I have presented complex information to a lot of people over the years. The best method I have found is showing them, doing it with them, and then having them do it or crawl, walk, and run, as we called it in the military. For example, if I need to teach you how to tie your shoe, I will start by showing you how I tie my shoe, then help you tie your shoe, and finally have you tie your own shoe. Typically, I will then have you go teach someone else how to do it because teaching others, in my opinion, is one of the best ways to assess that you know something.

- **Describe a time you used your communication skills effectively to make a point.**

  I dealt with an aggressive patient with Alzheimer's who was in and out of our reality for much of each day. This patient had a habit of attacking nurses and trying to get out of his bed, so several of us nurses would take turns sitting near his bedside to try to keep him in bed and keep him from hurting himself. One night, as I was sitting there, the patient woke out of a dead sleep and yelled "There's a fire on the wall," while pointing to the bathroom sink. I didn't see any signs of a fire, but the patient insisted the whole room was on fire and told me to get the fire extinguisher. I asked the patient why he needed the fire extinguisher, and he looked at me with an evil smile and said "So I can bash your head in with it," which seemed a little concerning at the time. Instead of running out of the room and yelling for help, I simply sat back down and continued asking the patient questions about the fire extinguisher until, finally, he became mentally exhausted and went back to sleep. After that day, I never had an issue with that patient again, and other nurses would call me in the room when he was attacking them because the patient seemed to listen to me each time. I have found when you are experiencing difficulty in communication, it's best to just ask questions to the other party and listen to what they have to say.

- **Tell me about a time you were effective in giving a workshop.**

I ran a workshop years ago for small business owners to teach them about sales funnels. The request from the non-profit organization was a long, death-by-PowerPoint presentation, but I knew that none of the business owners would truly understand the information if it was just slides. Instead, I brought in bags of candy and I asked all of the business owners to come and stand in a line and each was given a bag of candy. I then explained that this was one long sales funnel, and we worked through each business owner stating a price for their bag of candy. It was the only time I have seen a $10-million bag of Reese's candy, but the end results were that the business owners had fun learning, and they retained the information years later when I ran into several of them at a conference.

- **Give an example of a time when you needed to speak up during a project and the outcome.**

I worked on a project with other teams, where my team was already strapped for human capital resources. The other teams had ample resources but were expecting my team to take on the majority of the work. I addressed this issue, citing the need for additional resources and asking the other team managers whether they were willing to part with their budget and send it my way. None of them wanted to share their budget, so ultimately, they decided to have their teams offload work from my team and the project moved forward to completion.

- **Can you tell me about a time you had to be assertive? What was the outcome?**

I once had an employee that would take a long time to do any project, but they had ample time to play on their phone. I attempted to give the employee training and other resources to help streamline project completion, but the issue was, ultimately, with their motivation to focus on projects. I sat the employee down and, essentially, told them we could work together to get things completed on time, or I would write them a letter of recommendation to find a new job. The employee then improved their focus to complete their tasks quickly, which still allowed them to have phone time during the day. It was a win-win for everyone involved.

- **Describe a time you used effective written communication to make a point.**

Many years ago, I worked with a hospice patient and was her only male nurse. The patient expressed some concerns about one of the other nurses because the patient felt this nurse didn't know how to do everything they should know how to do. Because of this, I provided the patient with my contact information. Early one morning, a few minutes before my shift, I was waiting outside of the patient's home in my vehicle when the patient sent me a text asking whether I was almost there because she had been without pain medication all night long and the nurse on duty didn't seem to know how to replace the medication bag. I quickly rushed into the patient's home to find the Morphine pump ringing in alarm that the medication bag was empty. I quickly changed the bag as per the physician's orders and the patient began receiving her pain medication. I then reported the issue to the hospice nursing company, which subsequently tried to sweep the incident under the rug because this patient was poor. My response was to send a letter to the State Board of Nursing to open an investigation, along with sending letters to other agencies. The result was that within 24 hours, investigators were interviewing the patient about her experience and the patient was able to get compensation for the incident. She was also able to switch to a new hospice nursing company.

- **Tell me about a challenge you faced while coordinating a project with other teams.**

The biggest challenge I have faced is getting other teams to complete their portion of the project on time. I have found that the best way to keep them on track is through scheduled check-ins, where we identify any blockers as a team and continue to reiterate why we are doing the project and how it benefits the team.

- **What have you done in your career to improve your verbal communication skills?**

With this question, the interviewer is trying to determine whether you are willing to continue your education and go outside of your comfort zone to advance your career.

To improve my verbal communication skills, I have taken several courses on public speaking and voice coaching. Additionally, I have volunteered for webinars and conference presentations to practice communicating with others.

- **How have you persuaded people with your documentation?**

  Yes. As a nurse, I had to use my assessment documentation of patients to persuade physicians to adjust medications or even to discharge patients when they were healthy enough to leave the hospital. My documentation had to be thorough enough to help the physicians make an educated decision about the patient's care.

- **What are the most challenging documents you have done?**

  I don't know that I have found any documents to be challenging, but if I have not done a specific type of document before, then I search online for an example template that helps me visualize the typical structure and layout of the document. From there, I organize my content into notes and then produce the document. If I had to select the most challenging documentation, I would suggest nursing notes because your documentation, literally, has life or death consequences for the patient. I witnessed this firsthand in the military when a nurse did not document properly, so the physician thought they needed to perform a procedure on the patient's other leg. Fortunately, the physician assistant spoke up and the physician reconfirmed the area for operation, so nothing bad happened to the patient.

- **What is your process for preparing written communication?**

  My process for preparing written communication is to identify the audience and the end objective. Then, I work my way back from there to ensure I have substantiation for why we need to get to that end objective and how it benefits anyone reading the documentation. My next step is to identify any possible objections the reader could have and the answers to those objections. Then, I create the documentation.

Conflict resolution

The following question assesses your ability to resolve conflicts in a way that benefits everyone involved:

- **Describe a time when you took accountability during a conflict with another person and how you resolved the conflict to benefit both parties.**

  In military training, I had one guy that just didn't like me for whatever reason, so we would end up in a lot of fistfights. One day, I approached him, and instead of using my fists to beat him up, I used my brain and we had a discussion about our careers and objectives with the training school. He never shared why he didn't like me initially, but after that day, we never had another fight or issue and went our separate ways after training.

Customer orientation

The following questions assess your ability to interact with clients:

- **Describe how you handle problems with customers?**

  I always start by listening to the customer to identify what the real issue is. Generally speaking, if you allow people to talk long enough, they will reveal the actual reason they are upset. Once I have identified the real issue, I can then work through possible solutions with the customer.

- **How do you go about establishing rapport with a customer? What have you done to gain their confidence? Give an example.**

  I have found that simplicity is better, so I start with a smile and a greeting when interacting with a customer. This approach defangs the customer, similar to how we might defang a malware sample to analyze it. When I worked in fast food and customers would verbally abuse me, I often found them coming back the next day to apologize and say their anger was not directed at me but rather at the situation they were going through in life.

  In one instance, a guy that spent almost an hour screaming that I was the devil for not giving him a free upgrade on his fry size came back a week later to tell me that he had buried his wife that day and was dealing with the emotions from that. It's important to approach customers with a positive attitude even if they are terrible to you because you can easily turn your haters into your biggest advocates. I've been in past situations where my boss has been yelling at me in front of customers, and customers who had literally been cursing me 10 minutes prior, coming up to my boss and telling them to leave me alone because I was doing such a great job. The fastest way to build rapport with customers in my opinion is to kill them with kindness and know what you are talking about. That will build trust quickly.

- **What have you done to improve relations with your customers?**

  I have done a number of things over the years, depending on what job I had. As a hospice nurse, I used to pay out of my own pocket for a rinse-less shampoo cap that I could use on bed-ridden patients to help them feel like they were able to take a real shower again. This was very popular with patient families, and it helped the patients have some dignity right before they passed away. When I worked as a janitor, I would give each client an upgraded cleaning package once a month, which meant an extra hour spent cleaning off the clock. Customers appreciated this extra touch, and when I left that company, I heard many of those customers tell the management team to double my wage to bring me back.

Decision making

The following questions are designed to assess your effective decision-making abilities:

- **Discuss an important decision you have made regarding a task or project at work. What factors influenced your decision?**

  As I'm writing this book, in one of my executive roles, I'm dealing with the decision of how we scale without some of the typical problems other EdTech companies have experienced. My decision-making process is to think at least 5 years ahead in terms of where I want the company and the cybersecurity community to be, then work backward from there. As a side note, it's always best with anything in life to start at the end and work backward from there. There are a number of factors that can influence my decision, but the major ones are budgetary and resource constraints. These constraints help me focus on the short-term wins I can get and what the longer-term roadmap needs to look like to get the company and community to achieve their 5-year objectives.

- **Have you ever made a poor decision at work? How did you recover?**

  Yes; I chose to help a fellow team member out and started helping them with their workload because they supposedly had a lot of personal issues going on. This led to them seeming to have perpetual personal issues and me doing all of their work while they were getting a paycheck much higher than mine. I recovered from this by just being direct with them and mentioning that I had been helping for several months, and if they had so many personal issues where they couldn't do their job, they need to speak to the management, or I would ask them about getting them some additional help. At the mention of the involvement of the management, this person's personal issues magically seemed to clear up and they started doing their tasks again.

- **Describe a time when you had to make a quick decision.**

  In the military, I had to make quick-shoot or no-shoot decisions. The key to being effective in decision-making under this kind of stress is to train a lot and always assess your training. Additionally, it is good to have others assess it to identify mistakes and offer suggestions about how you can make corrections and improve. In my opinion, the biggest part of decision-making is taking ownership of your decisions, good or bad. For example, if I cleared a room but some of my shots went into the hostage target, I need to take ownership of that and work to improve it, not blame other soldiers, the wind, or a rainy day as the cause. It was my decision to put rounds on that target, so I need to own that because it's the only way for me to improve my skills for a real-life scenario with that same hostage.

- **Can you provide an example of a time when you didn't have enough information to make a decision? What did you do?**

We might not have enough information at the time to make the best decision, but I am a firm believer that we can make a decision with whatever information we have, whether it is a good decision or a bad one. An example of when I didn't have enough information to make a good decision was while doing some trail running in a park with some friends and one of them became separated from the group. None of us had been to this park before, so rather than turning around and going back the way we came, as most people would do, we decided it would be best to go down a partially hidden trail that looked like it had not been used in years. For about 10 minutes, we walked along this trail and, finally, came out into a ravine, where the only way out was either back down that trail or to climb up a sheer rock cliff of about 70 feet, at about a 90-degree angle, without any rock climbing gear. Again, we naturally chose not to use common sense and decided to attempt to climb up the rock cliff. My friend was approximately 100 lbs heavier than me and a foot taller, so again, it made perfect sense to send him up the rock cliff first with me following. As we climbed the cliff, he kept losing his grip and kicked me in the face a few times, causing me to lose grip and, each time, almost sending me tumbling to my death below. We finally made it up the cliff and, after a short time, found another trail and, eventually, our friends. If I had more information regarding the park, I could have made a better decision on the route to go to find our friends. If I had more information regarding how difficult it was to climb a 70-foot rock cliff with no climbing gear, I would have been able to make a better decision about turning back to the trail versus climbing the rock cliff.

- **What is your process of determining how to handle a difficult customer?**

The first step is to always listen to the customer to identify what the real issue is and not just respond to comments they are making. Another key part is remaining calm and not getting emotional with the customer, so you can diffuse the situation. From there, I progress to identifying how I can solve problems for the customer, including what solutions can be implemented immediately and what other solutions might take some additional time or resources to implement.

- **What is your process of making important decisions?**

I make important decisions by thinking of the end result I want to achieve. Then, I work my way backward from there. Next, I identify anything that might be a blocker to a successful outcome and correlate all of the data I have to make the best decision. It is important for me to not be emotionally tied to the outcome of any decision I make.

- **How do you involve your manager or others when you make a decision?**

  Effective communication is the key to a successful career. I include my management team and other stakeholders in decision-making by, first, identifying who on the team needs to know about the decision. Then, I communicate a description of the decision and why it needs to be made. Additionally, I ask for the other person's objective thoughts on the decision. I always refrain from sharing my thoughts or opinions because I want to get honest feedback from the other party.

- **What is your process for identifying whether a decision you make is beneficial?**

  The decisions I make have clear objectives and **key performance indicators (KPIs)**. I track these to determine whether the decision I made has the beneficial impact intended.

- **Tell me about a time you had to defend your decision successfully even though key stakeholders were initially opposed to your decision.**

  One time, I received significant pushback on implementing a security awareness training program across the enterprise. I met with each stakeholder to identify any concerns they had and how they felt the program could benefit their department. I found many of the stakeholders shared the same concern in that their employees would not find the training relevant to their daily workflow, so I made sure that the program included scenarios across all departments and how a cyber attack could impact daily tasks for everyone. Ultimately, the program was approved and implemented, and it helped to reduce the risky behavior of end users across all departments. A key to the success of this project was communicating with stakeholders to identify their needs first and adjusting the program accordingly versus just creating a program and telling them that my way was their only option.

- **Which types of decisions do you make rapidly? And which types take you longer? Please provide examples.**

  An example of a decision I make rapidly is adjusting a training module to ensure students are retaining the skills they have learned. If I notice students have difficulty grasping a topic, I don't continue delivering the content in the same way with the same examples. Instead, I work to identify an explanation that they relate to and take the necessary time to ensure retention.

Decisions that take me longer to complete include analyzing employee performance reviews for raises. I like to digest not just the KPIs but also have a short meeting with the individual so that I can identify their needs. This way, instead of just giving someone a raise, I might also identify that they are working on a college degree, and then I can go fight to get a budget increase for more tuition assistance and distribute that economic opportunity across the entire team.

- **Describe a problem you have had when coordinating technical projects.**

The main challenge I have faced in coordinating technical projects is managing the different personalities of all team members.

- **What was your most difficult decision in the last 6 months and why was it difficult?**

The most difficult decision I have faced in the past 6 months was to cut staff hours back at a critical time when we needed all of the help we could get on projects. I had to reduce spending on the budget in the short term to keep the company financially viable for a longer period of time. This meant reducing the hours of some contractors we were working with on projects and investing my own time to cover the slack. Any good leader finds it challenging to make the decision to cut hours or positions because we understand the impact that can have on the individual on the receiving end.

- **Can you tell me your process for making highly technical decisions?**

For any decision, I focus on the end result and then identify the KPIs that are needed at each stage of the project to get me to that end result. I remove my emotional attachment to the outcome of the decision. Next, I perform a self-analysis of my skillset to determine whether I need to hire an additional resource to cover the technical skills needed for the project.

Delegation

The following questions assess your ability to delegate tasks to others:

- **Do you consider yourself a macro or micromanager?**

I consider myself a macro manager. I focus on hiring the best teams, providing a little direction on the ultimate objectives, and then step back to let these intelligent and creative people do their work. This approach leads to innovative ideas that drive massive revenue for the organization. Micromanagers cause your company to lose revenue and lose its best talent.

- **How do you make the decision to delegate work to your team?**

I know my own strengths and weaknesses and time constraints along with the strengths and weaknesses of my team members. This allows me to quickly delegate parts of a project to team members that specialize in those areas and own my own specialties.

For any aspiring manager reading this book, I suggest you study personality types, behavioral assessments, and human psychology so that you can also learn to read your team and empower them to peak performance.

- **What was the biggest mistake you have had when delegating tasks?**

Early in my career, the biggest mistake I made was delegating tasks to anyone. I quickly learned that I needed to know the strengths and weaknesses of my team members, so I could delegate the right tasks to the right people.

- **Can you tell me about your biggest success when delegating tasks?**

My biggest success when delegating tasks was to let a team member know the end outcome that we were looking for and then give them ample time to be creative. This team member came back having invented new technology that saved the company millions of dollars in just the first year of implementation.

Detail orientation

The following questions are designed to assess your attention to detail:

- **Describe a situation where you had an option to leave the details of a project to someone else or handle them yourself and what your decision was and why.**

This decision depends a lot on the project and the strengths of the team. One example is when I was tasked with building custom labs for a company. I had significantly more experience than my team in designing and building labs, so I chose to handle the details of the project and then collaborated with the team to get additional thoughts on ways to improve the lab design. The outcome of this approach was that we were able to create labs the company loved, which were delivered months before they expected them.

- **Reflecting back on previous jobs, overall, have those jobs required low attention to detail, a moderate amount of attention, or a high amount of detail to be successful in the job?**

  It really depends on the job, but the vast majority of positions I have held required a high level of detail. An example of this was when I worked as a nurse and had to document my patient assessments for the physician. If I did not perform the job properly and missed a detail, it could literally mean the difference between life and death for the patient.

- **Can you share a situation where you found it challenging to handle the details of a project?**

  I have not found it challenging to handle the details of any projects in my career.

  For this question though, you could share a situation where you found the details or instructions on a project challenging. A key takeaway for an interview is to never make up any situation just to answer a question. If you don't have an example to share for each question, it's okay.

- **Can you describe a situation where you found attention to detail was not important?**

  I find attention to detail extremely important to a successful outcome on projects. So, unfortunately, I do not have an example of this. For those reading this book, it is completely fine for you not to have an answer to this question because you believe in quality work. As a hiring manager, I look for people that strive to deliver quality work.

Employee development

This question is designed to assess your ability to build out employee development training:

- **Have you ever developed or enhanced a training program? If yes, please tell me your process for building one.**

  Yes, I have developed and enhanced several training programs in my career. My process varies slightly based on whether the program exists already and just needs to be improved or whether I am building it from scratch.

  For programs that require improvement, I will go through the training from the eyes of the trainee and identify what is working well in the program and what could be improved. Then, I outline a roadmap for improvements and projected costs, so I can fight for the necessary budget.

For programs that I am building from scratch, I start by performing a competitor analysis to identify issues with other programs so that we can solve those challenges in ours. Then, I outline a roadmap with projected costs and petition for the budget.

Evaluating alternatives

The following questions are designed to assess your process for evaluating alternate options:

- **Describe a situation where you had multiple options to choose from. How did you reach a decision about which options to choose?**

  With multiple options, I always perform trade-off analysis to determine the benefits and drawbacks of each decision. An example of this is when I had to decide how to reduce my team's spend over a few months. The initial choices I had were to either cut staff or to reduce the hours of some members of staff. I performed a trade-off analysis of each option and determined the best route was to reduce billable hours for a small number of contractors and retain full-time staff members.

- **Were there any alternate options you developed as part of your review process?**

  Yes; an alternate cost-saving option I identified was to reduce hours from the contract video editing team. This allowed me to keep one of the curriculum contractors working for a longer period of time.

- **Can you share a major decision you have made in the past 12 months and how you evaluated the other options that were available?**

  A major decision I have made in the past year is around my *Cyber Life* television show. Initially, I had contracted a media distribution company, but that company failed to deliver on the contract. I knew the owners of the company, so I had to determine whether I should cut the contract and terminate the relationship with these individuals or remain with them but not get anything in the contract fulfilled. I did my due diligence and assessed competitors in the space and, ultimately, decided to terminate the contract and move to another distribution company, which has led to a massive increase in viewership for my show and proper distribution.

- **Are there types of decisions that you find more difficult to make than others?**

  For me, the toughest decisions are always around cutting staff members because of budget reasons. Any decision like this has an impact on the individual and their family. Some executives look at team members as just a number on a spreadsheet, but I always see the human behind the number. If I do have to lay off people, I work hard to find them something within my network prior to their last day with my company.

Flexibility

The following questions are designed to assess your flexibility on the job:

- **Have you ever had a subordinate whose performance was consistently below average? What did you do to improve their performance?**

  Yes; I have come across several of these individuals over the years and found that it's best to start with something positive they are doing. Then, I ask them what they think could be improved and shut up to let them talk. If they have no suggested improvements, I share my thoughts and work with them to identify whether we can add some training to help them improve or utilize another method. In a few rare cases, the person simply didn't want to be there and didn't want to improve, so I had to fire them.

- **Describe how you make adjustments to your management approach if you see it's not working to improve performance.**

  I look for parts of my approach that are working and double down on those. Also, I assess the personality type of the other person and adjust my communication approach to be more in line with their personality type.

- **What is your process for working through obstacles that you face in projects?**

  My process is simple: I focus on the end result I want and remain persistent until I reach my goal. Usually, persistence is the main key to success in both projects and life.

- **Describe your process when you experience difficulty persuading someone else to your point of view.**

  If someone continues to be resistant to my point of view, I always ask them to share why they feel that way. This helps me identify real objections and determine a response for each objection. If the other party continues to be resistant, I might bring in a mediator to listen to both sides and help us talk through a solution.

Follow-up and control

The following questions are designed to assess your process for tracking metrics:

- **What is your process for tracking projects that you have delegated to others?**

  I like to give my team members autonomy in how they complete a project. So, my typical tracking is an informal check-in with a team member to ensure we are hitting key milestones within the project. This check-in might be done via email or a messenger service such as Slack or Discord, with an option to speak on the phone if the team member has questions. Over the years, I have tried different methods, and I have found that if I hire very smart people and give them autonomy, the projects always get done on time, within budget, and the team member usually invents a new process or product as a result of having the freedom to choose how to spend their time to get us to the end objective.

- **What is your process for collecting data for performance reviews?**

  I have a few task-based checklists that I use for performance reviews. I just complete these on a weekly basis so that I have enough data when it is time to make determinations regarding salary increases.

- **Describe your method for tracking tasks assigned to your team.**

  To track tasks assigned to our overall team, I use project management software to track each task and who is responsible for the task completion. I build milestone check-ins into every project to ensure the team stays on track for completion.

- **What key metrics were you held to in your last position?**

  In a past position, a key metric was the number of content hours produced in a given month. Another key metric was staying below budget while scaling.

Initiative

The following questions are designed to assess your initiative:

- **Describe a situation where you anticipated problems and were able to influence a new direction to avoid those problems.**

  A recent example of anticipating problems and pivoting direction is when I noticed a lab host provider had limited capabilities for us to build advanced cybersecurity labs with standard industry tools while leveraging our proprietary technology stack. I worked with my team to identify the cost ranges of building our own architecture and performed a trade-off analysis of both options. As I write this book, the company is in the midst of pivoting toward owning its own lab platform to build advanced labs.

- **How were you assigned tasks in your last role?**

  In my last role, I was given a list of content that needed to be built over the next year and then was responsible for identifying security professionals that were skilled to create that content.

- **What excited you the most about your last position?**

  The opportunity to work with team members all over the world.

- **Describe a time when you developed a project that went above and beyond the requirements of your job description.**

  Several years ago, I had started a new job, and as part of their onboarding process, I rotated between departments so that I could get a more holistic view of what everyone in the company did in their day-to-day operations. In one department, I noticed that the current training they had on one of the software applications was extremely boring, and this sentiment was shared by that entire team. I spent the next weekend building a new training program for that department and then proposed the idea to their manager after the content was built. They loved the new training and implemented it that same week.

- **Can you share a time in school when you exceeded expectations?**

  During the first semester of my undergraduate degree program, my spouse had to be hospitalized and I missed several weeks of classes. The dean of the campus met with me and asked whether I could complete my missing assignments and finish the semester with a passing grade. I not only completed the missing assignments, but I also did extra credit assignments and ended up with perfect grades that semester, winning an award from the university.

Interpersonal skills

The following questions are designed to assess your interpersonal skills:

- **Describe a recent unpopular decision you made and what the outcome was.**

  A recent unpopular decision I made was the decision to reduce contractor hours for a short period of time. After making the decision, I communicated it to the contractors and explained why we had to make the cut in the short term, which they understood.

- **Can you share an example of the most difficult person you have ever worked with and how you handled your interactions with them?**

  Back when I worked in fast food, there was an employee that refused to do any work when he was on shift. He would also horseplay and throw trash all over the restaurant. I mostly kept my cool, but one day I confronted him and mentioned that if he didn't like his job he could just quit and make it easier on the rest of us. He then shared how he needed this job to pay his bills, and I mentioned that it might make sense for him to start doing the job, so he could keep it. I was not in his chain of command at all, but this conversation seemed to work and he became one of the top employees at the restaurant.

- **Describe how you contributed to a team environment in your last position.**

  In my last role, I focused on the mission of the company and the performance outcomes we wanted across the organization. While working on projects with different teams, I focused on being respectful of the thoughts and opinions of others and recognizing their individual contributions to projects. The collaboration between teams allowed the company to scale without a significant increase in cost.

Innovation

The following questions are designed to assess your ability to innovate with new ideas to solve problems:

- **Describe a situation where you had to be innovative at work. What was the outcome?**

  As a nurse, I had a challenge with one baby I worked with where, during feeding time, he would roll around and try to pull out his feeding tube and knock over the syringe used for feeding him. One of my hands would be occupied holding the syringe and the other pouring food in the syringe, so I would have to try and block the baby with my arms as he tried to pull out the tube. One day out of frustration, I went through his equipment and pieced together a new device that could be used to vent (in the medical field, it's commonly called gastric decompression) the patient's feeding tube prior to the feeding and allow food to be delivered, all while remaining hands-free for me. I called the pediatric physician and explained what I had built and then received an order from her to deliver food via my new device at the next feeding time. When I tested the new device, I found I could keep both hands free during the feeding, which allowed me to use a toy to distract the child. Later, I ended up doing a provisional patent application on the device and selling the rights to a large healthcare company.

- **Describe a time you made a suggestion for improvement to your boss. What was the end result of the conversation?**

  I noticed my manager seemed to have reservations about communicating in meetings with other department heads and that the managers of the other departments seemed to ignore her on the few occasions she decided to speak up on a matter. I sat down with this manager and asked her whether she had noticed similar treatment from the other department managers and asked how she felt the situation could be improved. Then, I shared my suggestions; one of those suggestions was to bring me as a champion to the meetings to reaffirm her point of view and gain buy-in from the other departments. At the next meeting, this manager shared her opinion on a topic and I mentioned it was a great idea and how I felt it could be applied on a broader scale. Having a second person reaffirm her point of view seemed to help as she quickly received buy-in from the other teams and no longer had issues in meetings moving forward.

- **Can you describe a time you used a non-traditional method to solve a problem on the job?**

  As a janitor, I worked the night shift. One evening, I noticed the facility I usually cleaned was out of cleaning solutions and the only cleaning product left was a bottle of dish soap. I let my management team know and then cleaned the facility using the dish soap, which worked much better than traditional cleaning solutions.

- **When was the last time you had to think "outside of the box"? How did you do it?**

  A recent example is building an entire 9-month custom cybersecurity training program in less than 2 months. Most cybersecurity programs focus on certifications, which makes it easy to just copy exam objectives and perform knowledge-based training to those objectives. With a custom, on-the-job task-focused program, you have to create all of the case studies and lab scenarios from scratch, build all of the content, and perform quality checks to ensure everything is working correctly. The keys to our success on this project were a talented curriculum team and moving fast to deliver the content.

- **Describe a time you were required to use creative thinking on the job to solve a problem.**

  At one healthcare company I worked at, we had an issue where patients would consistently show up late for their medication appointments. They stated they did not know what to expect during the treatment, even though most of them came multiple times per week and had been given brochures. I decided to create a series of short videos for these patients, which were entertaining and fun, and walked them through what to expect during their appointment, reminding them how important it was to show up at their scheduled time. Within a few weeks, these simple videos led to a reduction in patients being late.

- **What is one of your most creative ideas?**

  Inventing the pediatric medical device is probably my most creative idea that has come to fruition so far since it was used to help a lot of children.

Integrity

The following questions are designed to assess your integrity:

- **Describe a time when you were asked to keep information confidential on the job.**

  When I worked in the military, I dealt with information at different levels of classification. The key to confidential or classified information is to understand the controls you need to follow for the protection and distribution of the information.

- **Describe a time you acted with integrity.**

  I worked with a hospice patient who experienced mental deterioration, which led to her withdrawing large amounts of cash from the bank and hiding it in her dresser drawers and other places around her house. This woman had two daughters: one daughter had legal custody, and the other daughter had no visitation rights. The daughter with legal custody told me that her sister was not allowed into the home and that if I found any money I should tell her about it. Later that night, after the sister with legal custody went to bed, the other sister showed up at the front door demanding entry into the home. She stated her mother had withdrawn money to help her pay her rent. I attempted to reach the sister with legal custody, but she did not answer my calls. So, I denied access to the other woman and mentioned I would be forced to contact law enforcement if she attempted to gain entry to the home. Finally, she went away and I began preparing the patient's medication. After preparing the medication, I washed my hands in the bathroom and searched for a towel to dry with. In the closet with towels, there was a stack of hundred-dollar bills that probably amounted to several thousand dollars. I called the daughter with legal custody again and left a message about finding the cash and mentioning exactly where it was. Early the next morning, that daughter came to retrieve the money to put it back into the bank account. She also thanked me for denying access to her sister. She explained her sister had a narcotics addiction, and that was why she didn't have the legal right to interact with their mother. She had robbed her mother a few times for drug money and had been charged with the crimes.

- **Can you tell me about a time when your trustworthiness was challenged and how you reacted?**

  I had a boss in fast food that accused me of damaging the walls of a small building we called the dog house in the drive-thru. In this small building, we would sit to collect payment after someone placed their order, and then the customer would move to the main building to pick up their food. The good news for me was the dog house was damaged while I was out of town and it had cameras inside, which captured another employee causing the damage. I reported my manager to their supervisor, who was head of the region, and they faced disciplinary action for accusing me before doing simple diligence to review the camera footage. Shortly after the accusation, I quit that job and went to an employer that appreciated my hard work ethic.

- **Describe a time when you witnessed dishonesty in the workplace and how you handled it.**

  I noticed another nurse one time writing out her entire nursing note for each day of the weekend on a Friday night. It was impossible for her to predict what the patient's condition would be over the next few days, and charting like that was against nursing standards of practice. At first, I addressed it directly with the nurse, but she told me she didn't care what I thought and she was going to do what she wanted. So, I ended up reporting it to the company and the state board of nursing. An investigation opened that found the nurse had been documenting in that way on several patients in the past. Additionally, it was found that the nurse was reporting hours for two separate companies on the same shift hours. The last I heard regarding the investigation was that it had been referred to the district attorney for criminal prosecution, along with a nursing board action to revoke her nursing license.

- **Describe a time you chose to trust someone on the job and the outcome.**

  As a nurse, I chose to trust another nurse to pick up medications for my patient from the pharmacy even though this nurse had ended his work shift. This nurse was trustworthy and returned with the patient's medication. I am still connected with the nurse to this day because he proved he was trustworthy.

Introducing change

The following questions are designed to assess your ability to implement change in an organization:

- **Describe your process for implementing policy changes to your team?**

  My process for implementing policy changes across the team is to start by explaining the policy at a high level and why we are implementing the policy. Then, I ask the team to surface any questions or concerns with the new policy so that we can address them. Finally, I continue checking in with the team after we implement the policy to ensure it is meeting its objectives and to ensure it is not causing significant disruption to the team's productivity.

- **Have you ever experienced resistance when implementing a new idea or policy with your team? If yes, what was your process for dealing with the resistance?**

  Yes; people inherently are resistant to change. I have found that the best way to combat resistance is to ensure people understand the why behind the new policy or idea and how it can directly benefit them.

Leadership

The following questions are designed to assess your leadership skills:

- **Describe some ways in which you motivate your co-workers.**

  I motivate team members in many ways. One simple method I used in the pre-pandemic days was to write a simple thank you card and leave them across desks at the organization. The majority of employees had no clue who was the person behind the random thank you cards, but it helped improve morale and increased productivity across the organization.

- **Can you share a time when two members of the team did not work well together and your process for motivating them to work together?**

  I had two employees who didn't like each other and were in a conflict, which was affecting their productivity. After trying standard solutions to resolve the issue, I wrote a number on the whiteboard and told them it was the bonus that would be split between the two of them each month. If there was any fighting or if work was not getting done, the number would reduce by $100 for each occurrence until it went back down to $0 for the month. Additionally, I mentioned that it was up to both of them to work together to get this bonus because this bonus couldn't be earned working as individuals. In the first month, they only earned $100 because they both kept fighting with each other, but when that $100 was paid out, they both realized the potential for earning a lot more. So, in the second month, it was a night and day difference in terms of their relationship, and they received the full bonus that month and in subsequent months.

- **Describe the toughest situation you have faced when trying to get cooperation from other teams.**

  The toughest situation I have experienced is just getting full buy-in from another team on the project. I have found the best way to get the buy-in from other teams is to ensure they see a clear benefit for their team in the project.

Listening

The following questions are designed to assess your ability to listen to others:

- **Describe a time when you made a mistake because you did not listen to the advice of others.**

  One time, I ignored advice from a close friend regarding a business deal. It led me to lose tens of thousands of dollars on a bad deal.

- **How do you show people that you are listening to them?**

  I use active listening, which means I listen to the person and engage in the conversation with them to let them know I am listening. My goal with this is to just have a conversation and not try to force my agenda onto them.

- **Describe when you think listening is important in your job and when you find it difficult to listen.**

  To me, active listening is always important in the job.

Motivation

The following questions assess your ability to motivate other people and self-motivation:

- **How do you motivate your team?**

  I motivate my team through many methods. It really depends on the individual and what they relate to the most. For example, I have some employees who are motivated when I sponsor someone else for a security certification because the employee was productive. I have other employees who also prefer direct recognition of their efforts.

- **Describe your process for assessing when your team members exceed your expectations on projects. How do you reward them?**

  I hire smart and creative people, so I always expect they will crush my expectations. I have not been let down yet. As far as processes for assessing expectations, I track the outcomes that we want in each project and the contributions of each team member. Then, I reward them appropriately.

- **Can you share how you get subordinates to work at their peak potential and produce at a higher level?**

  If people truly believe in the objectives, then they will naturally produce at high levels. Hire the best and empower them to be even better, and your company can be unstoppable.

- **Can you share a time when you were able to have a positive impact on others?**

  I worked with a little boy who was from a very poor family. So, with the permission of his parents, I would treat the little kid to ice cream and fast food, along with his family, so he could experience different things from poverty. I grew up very poor, so I saw myself in this little kid. I also took this kid to a fire station to meet firefighters and see the trucks, and he could not stop talking about that experience for almost a month.

- **How do you define success in your career?**

  To me, success is defined as impact. What kind of impact am I having on the world? That's real success to me.

Negotiation

The following questions assess your experience negotiating:

- **Can you share the most difficult negotiation you were involved in and the results of that negotiation?**

  A while back, I was involved in a massive business deal, where the other party was determined to make it a deal that only benefited them. We were successful in finding some middle ground and all parties walked away happy with the deal.

- **Describe a time when you had to bargain with someone. What was your process?**

  I bargained with my Spanish language teacher to not only receive training but also have her do some translation work for my television show. The process was simple in that I, first, closed the deal for having her train me. Then, I focused on negotiating to add in some translation work for the show.

- **What do you find to be the most difficult part of negotiation?**

  When I first started negotiating, the most difficult part was identifying what the outcome I wanted would look like. Once I created the vision in my head of exactly what I wanted, it became much easier to get what I wanted in the negotiation.

Organizational responsibilities

The following questions assess your ability to prioritize organizational responsibilities:

- **Describe a time when you had to make a difficult choice between your personal and professional life.**

  I am involved in several start-up companies, which eat up a lot of my time. The difficult choice I had to make is sacrificing watching movies and television shows so that I can focus that time on those businesses.

- **How do you decide what is the top priority when you schedule your time?**

  I focus on what the most impactful project will be to the organization, especially to drive revenue growth or cost savings, and focus on that.

- **Describe what you do when you experience interruptions to your planned schedule.**

  I simply adapt to the interruptions and reprioritize my tasks to ensure I am only focused on the most critical tasks that will have the biggest impact.

Performance management

The following questions assess your performance management ability:

- **Describe a time you helped someone accept change and make the necessary adjustments to move forward. What were the change/transition skills that you used with this person?**

    The largest change I have helped others accept is a transition from military service back to civilian life. As far as process goes, I just shared my own journey of transitioning, the mindset changes that need to happen, and the challenges I faced when getting out of the military.

- **Describe how you have empowered others into accomplishing tasks.**

    I empower others by using social engineering tactics to convince people that they can accomplish the tasks they are trying to achieve and by mentoring them through that transition journey.

- **Describe your process for handling performance reviews.**

    I approach performance reviews by looking holistically at the person to identify not only how they are performing on projects but whether there are any challenges or personal issues happening that might have led to lower productivity.

- **Can you tell me about a time you had to take disciplinary action against one of the people you supervised?**

    Yes; I have had to do write-ups for performance issues and terminate some employees. However, my process is to first meet with the employee and attempt to identify any training opportunities that we can invest in to help the employee. Then, I move into more formal disciplinary action if needed.

- **Give an example of how you provide constructive criticism to your team.**

    One example is mentioning a positive thing an employee has done on a project and then offering your suggestions to help improve the project.

Behavioral interview questions are asked in every interview that I have ever been in and they are one of the easiest types of questions to prepare for because you are answering with your real life stories.

Summary

In this chapter, you learned about common behavioral questions that you might be asked in an interview. Remember, even if you don't have work situations that you can use as examples to answer these questions, you still have experiences from your personal life that you can use to answer them. In an interview, you will probably only be asked a few of these questions, but it's good to study a few questions from each section so that you are well prepared for interviews.

In the next chapter, the authors will share their final interview advice with you.

13
Final Thoughts

In this chapter, we (the authors) share our final thoughts and advice on cybersecurity interviews and careers.

The following topics will be covered in this chapter:

- Chris Foulon's final thoughts and advice
- Tia Hopkins' final thoughts and advice
- Ken Underhill's final thoughts and advice

Chris Foulon's final thoughts and advice

Congratulations! You have made it to another milestone on your journey towards your cybersecurity career. Notice that I didn't say that you *arrived at the end* because it is not the end; it is just the beginning! This milestone is just the beginning of what I am hoping will be a long cybersecurity career journey for you, where you learn daily, give back to others even if you are only a step ahead, and help make the world a safer place. I am hoping you will take the lessons learned from this book to help get that role you are looking for and positively impact those around you!

Cybersecurity is such an evolving field, and we need people from various backgrounds and diverse points of view to tackle the growing cybersecurity problems. Take the passion you have and share it with others, whether that might be at your child's PTA group, group of friends, or just your local school system. Please help the next generation prepare for it as well!

In writing these final thoughts for you today, I say you can do it! I received this message from a connection of mine that also demonstrated my journey:

"Chris - I hope all is well. I have been following your journey since we connected back in 2016, and I commend your persistence and intentionality in going after your career goals. You willed yourself into cybersecurity and are now a thought leader in the space.

Best,

James Jackson"

Connect with Chris on LinkedIn: `https://www.linkedin.com/in/christophefoulon`.

Tia Hopkins' final thoughts and advice

You made it to the end of the book! Nice! There's no greater investment than the investments you make in yourself. I'm sure Ken and Chris will give you some incredible tips and words of encouragement to take with you, so I'm going to do my best to keep up with them by leaving a few of my personal mottos and beliefs I'm hoping will help you throughout your cybersecurity career journey.

First, know your *why*. Before you go down the path of investing in education and certification training, go back to step zero and ask yourself, *Why am I here?*, *Why do I even want to pursue a career in cybersecurity?*, and *Am I sure this is where I want to be and not just a career someone told me would be good to pursue?*

Cybersecurity careers can be incredibly rewarding, but I won't pretend for a second that it's easy. Knowing your *why* will continue to guide you, balance you, keep you sane when things get hard (and they absolutely will), and motivate you if you get down on yourself and begin questioning your capabilities. If you don't know why you've chosen this industry, then you're allowing everyone else to define what your career should look like. For example, if you ask someone whether you should pursue a degree or certification, many people will give you an answer based on their opinion and personal experiences. But the right answer is, *it depends*. It depends on *your* desired outcomes and what you want for *your* career – not what worked for someone else in theirs.

My next point... I played tackle football for a number of years and learned a lot about the game and myself. I was at practice one night going through a linebacker drill and I was struggling with the technique. I tried over and over again to the point where I got so frustrated that I had to take a break. Finally, I took a deep breath, tried again, and I got it right. I absolutely nailed it! I was so happy. But when I looked over at my coach in search of a smile or some other sign of approval, he wasn't smiling. He didn't nod or even tip his cap. Instead, he looked at me and said, *"Don't just do it till you get it right; do it till you can't get it wrong."* Admittedly, I was incredibly annoyed at the time, but after practice, I thought about it and it made perfect sense. Since that day, I've carried his message with me, and even today, it influences my work ethic. So, my message to you is, when you're learning a new skill or concept, don't just practice until you get it right; practice until you can't get it wrong. Trust me when I tell you you'll stand out amongst your peers and be the go-to person in the room if you adopt this way of thinking. On the path to greatness, good enough should never be good enough.

Finally, I want to leave you with sort of an affirmation I created for myself a while back. Sometimes, we work so hard to achieve our goals that we are too hard on ourselves and push a bit more than we should. I'm guilty of this as well so I've recently developed the habit of reminding myself to give myself grace. From my perspective, G.R.A.C.E. is a package deal, and on certain days I have to embody some of these mindsets more than others, but the total package keeps me grounded. I'll share its contents with you:

- **G**rit:

    - Official definition: The passion and perseverance for long-term and meaningful goals.

    - Tia's translation: DON'T QUIT.

- **R**esilience:

    - Official definition: The ability to recover from a setback, adapt well to change, and keep going in the face of adversity.

    - Tia's translation: ALWAYS GET UP.

- **A**gility:

    - Official definition: The ability to think and understand quickly.

    - Tia's translation: BE QUICK ON YOUR FEET.

- Curiosity:

  - Official definition: A strong desire to learn or know something.

  - Tia's translation: NEVER STOP LEARNING.

- Empowerment:

  - Official definition: The knowledge, confidence, means, or ability to do things or make decisions for yourself.

  - Tia's translation: ASK FOR FORGIVENESS, NOT PERMISSION.

Your career is your choice and your responsibility. Find your lane, and if you can't find one, create one. Use this book as a tool to help you find and land the job that's right for you – because *you* said so. Good luck!

Connect with Tia on LinkedIn: `https://www.linkedin.com/in/yatiahopkins`.

Ken Underhill's final thoughts and advice

First, congratulations on making it to the end of the book. You have worked hard, and preparing for your job interview is just the beginning of a rewarding career. I have seen some people across social media telling others to *fake it until you make it* for job interviews. My advice is to ignore them because a hiring manager can always see through the lie. Instead, if you don't know the answer to something, just say you don't know but that you know how to go find the answer. Remember, nobody in cybersecurity knows every single nook and cranny of cybersecurity, so we all do Google searching from time to time.

Another mistake I see people making is not networking properly. Remember, relationships are a two-way street so it's important to give to the other person instead of just expecting to take. In the context of using networking to get job interviews, instead of reaching out to someone on LinkedIn and saying *Please, please help me get a job interview*, try instead asking whether they need help with any projects so you can build your skills, or ask them whether you can help them in any other way. Building real relationships will accelerate your career. In fact, a young woman focused on building a real relationship with me via LinkedIn and Zoom. She had applied to jobs for months, hearing nothing back, but when she connected with me, I was able to connect her with a company that was hiring and she aced the interview. She now works at a fantastic company with a salary she never dreamed of getting as an entry-level cybersecurity professional and this all happened within 2 weeks.

Regarding the debate on certifications versus college degrees versus just learning skills on your own, I will say *it depends*. I'm not a fan of certifications but I am fully aware that some companies require those or college degrees for jobs. I would suggest reflecting on what career you want to do and which companies you want to work at, then deciding which (if any) certifications or college degrees you need. The other thing to keep in mind is that almost everything in a job description is just part of a wish list. If you see that you have a few of the skills listed, then apply for the job. The worst-case scenario is that they say no or you never hear back about an interview. That is totally fine, and you just move on to the next company. Remember, every *no* is one step closer to your *yes*, and sometimes doors close in life because a really awesome opportunity is just around the corner for you.

I recommend you take the latest interview appointment time they have available, so you remain in the interviewer's mind. There is a concept called *recency bias*, which just means recent events in the person's mind are given more importance than past events. By having your interview be the last one of the day, you will be in the interviewer's mind as they make the hiring decision.

I also recommend that you create a short slide presentation for job interviews. This will help you stand out from all other candidates. The presentation should be about five slides maximum, and the first slide should outline your understanding of why they need someone (you) in this job. You will need to do research on the company and probably speak to some of their employees to get the information for the first slide.

The next three slides should show your 30, 60, and 90-day plans for what you are going to do once you are hired to help the organization reach its goals. And the final slide should have your name, a tagline, and a short bulleted list of the key skills that you have for the job. Creating this presentation helps plant the seed in the interviewer's mind that you already have the job and have a plan of action, plus it gives them a short summary in the bulleted list of why you are the most qualified person for the job.

When you reach the end of your job interview, the interviewer typically asks whether you have any questions. I suggest you then ask the interviewer whether you have given them enough information for them to make an offer. If they say no, then ask them what additional information they are needing from you.

The final thought I will leave you with is my technique for passing exams and interviews over the years. I would simply take a piece of paper and a pen and write out exactly what I wanted to happen during the exam or interview as if it had already happened. This may seem too simple to work, but it has always worked for me.

As an example, if I wanted a job as a SOC analyst I would write *"The interview for the SOC analyst job went great. They didn't ask me any difficult questions and it felt more like a conversation with friends than it did an interview. I was excited to receive their offer within a week after the interview."*

The people that consistently struggle to find their first job in cybersecurity do not follow this manifestation approach and the other information shared in this book. You can be like them and try applying to thousands of jobs and hope to hear back or you can take the road less traveled and apply the knowledge you have gained in this book to help you get your dream career faster.

The choice is yours.

Connect with Ken on LinkedIn: `https://www.linkedin.com/in/kenunderhill`.

Summary

Congratulations! You made it to the end of this book, but not the end of your career journey. In this book, you learned common interview questions for a variety of cybersecurity careers, you learned about the most common behavioral interview questions asked, and how you can *hack* yourself.

Index

Symbols

A

B

Packt.com

Subscribe to our online digital library for full access to over 7,000 books and videos, as well as industry leading tools to help you plan your personal development and advance your career. For more information, please visit our website.

Why subscribe?

- Spend less time learning and more time coding with practical eBooks and Videos from over 4,000 industry professionals

- Improve your learning with Skill Plans built especially for you

- Get a free eBook or video every month

- Fully searchable for easy access to vital information

- Copy and paste, print, and bookmark content

Did you know that Packt offers eBook versions of every book published, with PDF and ePub files available? You can upgrade to the eBook version at packt.com and as a print book customer, you are entitled to a discount on the eBook copy. Get in touch with us at customercare@packtpub.com for more details.

At www.packt.com, you can also read a collection of free technical articles, sign up for a range of free newsletters, and receive exclusive discounts and offers on Packt books and eBooks.

Other Books You May Enjoy

If you enjoyed this book, you may be interested in these other books by Packt:

Operationalizing Threat Intelligence

Kyle Wilhoit, Joseph Opacki

ISBN: 9781801814683

- Discover types of threat actors and their common tactics and techniques
- Understand the core tenets of cyber threat intelligence
- Discover cyber threat intelligence policies, procedures, and frameworks
- Explore the fundamentals relating to collecting cyber threat intelligence
- Understand fundamentals about threat intelligence enrichment and analysis
- Understand what threat hunting and pivoting are, along with examples
- Focus on putting threat intelligence into production
- Explore techniques for performing threat analysis, pivoting, and hunting

Cybersecurity Career Master Plan

Dr. Gerald Auger, Jaclyn "Jax" Scott, Jonathan Helmus, Kim Nguyen

ISBN: 9781801073561

- Gain an understanding of cybersecurity essentials, including the different frameworks and laws, and specialties
- Find out how to land your first job in the cybersecurity industry
- Understand the difference between college education and certificate courses
- Build goals and timelines to encourage a work/life balance while delivering value in your job
- Understand the different types of cybersecurity jobs available and what it means to be entry-level
- Build affordable, practical labs to develop your technical skills
- Discover how to set goals and maintain momentum after landing your first cybersecurity job

Packt is searching for authors like you

If you're interested in becoming an author for Packt, please visit `authors.packtpub.com` and apply today. We have worked with thousands of developers and tech professionals, just like you, to help them share their insight with the global tech community. You can make a general application, apply for a specific hot topic that we are recruiting an author for, or submit your own idea.

Share Your Thoughts

Now you've finished *Hack the Cybersecurity Interview*, we'd love to hear your thoughts! Scan the QR code below to go straight to the Amazon review page for this book and share your feedback or leave a review on the site that you purchased it from.

`https://packt.link/r/1801816638`

Your review is important to us and the tech community and will help us make sure we're delivering excellent quality content.

Made in the USA
Monee, IL
06 September 2022

13420793R00144